THE EIGHTH DAY & TOTO THE HERO

THE EIGHTH DAY
&
TOTO THE HERO
Jaco Van Dormael

translated by
Pierre Hodgson

faber and faber
LONDON · BOSTON

First published in 1996
by Faber and Faber Limited
3 Queen Square London WC1N 3AU

Photoset by Parker Typesetting Service, Leicester
Printed in England by Clays Ltd, St Ives plc

Jaco Van Dormael is hereby identified as author of this work in accordance with
Section 77 of the Copyright, Designs and Patents Act 1988

A CIP record for this book
is available from the British Library
ISBN 0–571–19037–5

2 4 6 8 10 9 7 5 3 1

CONTENTS

Jaco Van Dormael

LIFE LESSONS
Jaco Van Dormael in Conversation with Pierre Hodgson
Rixensart, September 1996

In January 1992, I conducted a detailed interview with Jaco Van Dormael about his first film, *Toto the Hero*. That conversation was published in 1993, in *Projections 2*. It appears in a somewhat abbreviated form later in this volume, as a preface to the English translation of the script of *Toto*.

Now, almost five years later, Jaco Van Dormael's second film, *The Eighth Day*, has just been released. Alongside Daniel Auteuil, the film stars Pascal Duquenne, an actor afflicted with Down's syndrome who appeared in *Toto* in a supporting role. A controversy over Van Dormael's use of a mentally handicapped actor to play a mentally handicapped character overshadowed the film's première at Cannes in May, and its subsequent French and Belgian releases. Vituperative comments in the French-language press had no apparent effect on the Cannes jury, which gave Daniel Auteuil and Pascal Duquenne joint best actor prize. Nor did they affect box-office results. People flocked to see *The Eighth Day* in their thousands. By European standards, the film is an expensive one, full of special effects, but it covered its costs in France and Belgium alone. It seems unlikely that the impact – or the controversy – will be quite so great in Britain and America, where the audience for foreign-language films is restricted, but with the Japanese, German and other continental releases yet to come, the film has already established itself as a commercial success. In that respect, its career is almost a mirror image of that of *Toto*, which generated an enormous amount of favourable criticism, though – as is the way with first feature films – it reached only a limited audience.

Almost five years after our first encounter, Jaco and I were commissioned to spend another full day together, discussing the making of *The Eighth Day*. It is a measure of how much has changed in Jaco's life that he has moved out of the centre of Brussels, where, in 1992, he was living in a kind of commune, to a house set in suburban woods some twenty miles outside town. I had not been to Belgium since our last conversation. The country has changed a great deal. A climate of serious political uncertainty provided a strong undercurrent to our discussion. Belgium is divided into two halves, one Flemish-speaking, the other French-speaking. Never very friendly, they are now at loggerheads. Furthermore, a paedophile scandal following the announcement that several children had been found murdered, erupted into a full-blown political and constitutional crisis, as politicians failed to react when policemen and examining magistrates accused each other of covering up various *affaires*, including the assassination of a former minister. Jaco Van Dormael's background is partly Flemish-speaking, partly French-speaking. Most, though not all, of his films have been in French, but, unlike many French-speaking Belgian film professionals, he has never chosen to work in France. I sensed that Belgium's collective crisis of confidence had affected him considerably. He speaks here of a desire to embark on a more private kind of film-making. For these and other reasons, the conversation which follows is perhaps more personal and less purely technical than our earlier discussion. I feel that, nevertheless, it provides some generous insights into the thinking of a highly original film-maker.

Pierre Hodgson

PIERRE HODGSON: *Like* Toto the Hero, The Eighth Day *is a dark film disguised as a comedy.*

JACO VAN DORMAEL: I'll have to think what to say about that. (*He laughs.*) The darkness and comedy are definitely characteristic of both films. I think most film-makers – most writers too for that matter – know that there are some things they want to develop and change from one work to the next and some things they'll never be able to make different. In *The Eighth Day* there are certain things I wanted to alter simply because I'd reached a different stage in my life. The idea of *Toto* was that its structure should function the way memory functions. I wanted the different bits of the jigsaw to come together in the character's memory. The story is designed around someone looking back on their lives, asking themselves what it's all been about. With this new film, I set out to do something in a completely different style. But then I realized it wasn't the style I wanted to change, it was the content. I wanted *The Eighth Day* to be about the present, to be set in the present tense. And that meant being a bit more impressionistic. It meant focusing on immediate sensations, like looking at flowers or noticing a particular scent. There's no past and no future involved, it's about living life as intensely as possible. *Toto* was about how the moment we're living now relates to the past and how it is going to turn into the future; questions one asks oneself at twenty-five or thirty. Now I'm more interested in simple pleasures, in what it feels like to be alive. And that's why *The Eighth Day* had to be told in a much simpler way. It had to be about its characters, about their moods. About emotion in general. The narrative structure only works in terms of emotion. The emotions are all that are told. It's a film about how emotions swell up and contradict each other. And that in turn leads to a heightening of the senses, for the characters, for me and for the audience.

PH: *In technical terms, how would you describe the narrative construction of* The Eighth Day?

JVD: The beginning, and the end – the two accounts of the Creation – are obviously there to bookend the film, to reassure me and satisfy my need for structure, and also to introduce the characters as quickly as possible. But whereas *Toto* is a dramatic structure, in which each part is essential and nothing can be removed without endangering the whole, *The Eighth Day* is more of an epic construction, organized as an accumulation of picaresque episodes, like *Don Quixote*, in which successive scenes need not necessarily contribute to the architecture of the whole. The point of each episode in *The Eighth Day* is in the episode itself, not in its relation to the rest. I took a great deal of pleasure in the making of scenes which were not dramatically significant, but which were emotionally powerful.

PH: *When we discussed* Toto, *years ago, you told me the meaning of a film was in its structure. Do you still believe that?*

JVD: Now I believe the meaning is in everyday life. I learnt that from people with Down's syndrome, from Pascal.[1] It's an idea that was present in my earlier work, but was somehow marginal to it. Before *Toto*, I made a short called *E Pericolo Sporgersi* which was equally complicated in terms of structure, but fifteen or sixteen

---

1 Pascal Duquenne plays the part of Georges. In *Toto the Hero*, he played the part of Célestin.

years ago I was making improvised films with mongoloids, with mentally handicapped people. My first attempt was a documentary on the Paralympics. I'd been brought up, very conventionally, to think you should never look mongoloids in the eye. I was told, if you look them in the eye, you'll embarrass them; they are unfortunates, they're often very unhappy, they feel different.

PH: *Did you know any Down's syndrome sufferers before you started working with them?*

JVD: No. It was a completely unfamiliar world. I'd intended to make a conventional documentary but they took over. As soon as a shot was set up, two of them would come and stand in front of the camera and say something totally surreal. That's how I discovered what fun they were. They just seemed to upset the best laid plans. And of course they loved making a film. Everything I'd been told about them was wrong. They loved being observed, they loved the camera and showing the world they existed. I found one or two who were natural born actors, so I decided to try them out on fiction. I made a short called *L'Imitateur*,[1] shot with a documentary crew. The script was a series of cue-cards, about forty in all, each containing one simple idea. And we improvised around each idea. That's how we made that film. Then they decided they wanted to go on acting, so they started working on theatre projects and they involved me in that work, which led to my meeting other handicapped actors. Working with them was a joy.

PH: *When we discussed* Toto, *you said that the big scene with Pascal on the lawn in front of the asylum was shot in a completely different way from the rest of the film, that it was improvised and that that had given you a great deal of freedom compared with the constraints you had laid upon yourself in the remainder of the film, which was very strictly written and storyboarded. But in* The Eighth Day *I have a feeling that some of that sense of freedom has gone. I feel that you have managed to turn Pascal into a full-blown professional, on a par with Daniel Auteuil.*

JVD: Regarding certain scenes, that is certainly true. Most of the film is shot as written. But even in the most written scenes, Pascal brings something unpredictable to the way he interprets his part. And, in any case, some of the film is entirely improvised. I was

---

1 *L'Imitateur:* The Imitator.

able to say to the crew, if it works, I'll put it in the film and if it doesn't, it doesn't matter. That's one of the advantages of a picaresque structure. It allowed me to try things out and then omit them if they didn't turn out right. But in fact, we included almost all the improvisation in the final cut. The scene in which Pascal dances alone in front of the television screens is one example. I just switched the music on and he went ahead and did his thing. In other instances, it's a question of *how* he does things. Like when he starts growling like a lion in the shoe shop. That wasn't in the script. The scene was written as a standard piece of comedy and he added that idea. It's true that I could have made the film with a much lighter crew and much more improvisation. But I'd already done that in the shorts. I didn't want *The Eighth Day* to have a documentary feel. Just because mentally handicapped people are out of the mainstream, it doesn't mean they can't be in mainstream films. On the contrary, I wanted them to be in the limelight. I'd done the experimental films. Now I had the freedom to do more or less as I pleased, I wanted to use that freedom to give them a main chance.

PH: The Eighth Day *is a much more political film than* Toto. *And the first time I saw the film, I was almost insulted by it, by the moment, for instance, when Pascal's character is told: 'You're better than the rest.' I thought you were saying people with Down's syndrome are from before the Fall and the rest of us are somehow wicked. Then when I saw the film a second time, I realized I was quite wrong, that wasn't what you were saying.*

JVD: Because it's his mother who says that to him.

PH: *But the social critique in the film is very forthright. And I'd like to know how central that is to what you were doing?*

JVD: I don't feel I'm about social criticism. I think I'm asking: what is it we are doing to our lives? The character of Georges, whom Pascal plays, is in each of us. He's the other we all keep hidden away in out hearts. Only his other isn't hidden. It's all he's got. My handicapped friends are entirely alienated, but part of me is alien too. It's a part of my personality which has been educated out of me. But when I'm with them, I really ask myself how I can do without it. Because they take such incredible pleasure in the moment, in eating and kissing, in touching things and giving someone a hug. They never think about the future, they never plan ahead. All that's been educated out of us. Our contact with the physical world is less and less real. We're helpless without the use of words. We ring people up, send faxes, watch TV, read the newspapers, all of which is supposed to broaden our horizons but actually diminishes our perception of others. We have a very narrow idea of what life is about. Unlike us, they have a relationship with the rest of the world which is physical, not virtual. They're interested in what they can touch and eat, in what is literally present. They live by the minute and that is very precious to me.

PH: *And if you were to make a third feature with handicapped actors, can you say whether that would be the reason for using them? Is the reason for using them that by watching them, we learn something about ourselves?*

JVD: Well at the moment, I don't feel like starting on another project. I feel like staying at home. But if I were to make another film now, I have a feeling I'd try and find a different way of making movies. I want to keep a camera here in the kitchen and stuff my fridge full of film stock. I want to go out and make a shot from time to time, in the same way as one writes scenes for a screenplay, without any notion of what the film might become in the end. I want to work without a completion bond. I want to shoot the trembling of a leaf or . . . (*Pause.*)

PH: *Is that a reaction to the cumbersomeness of commercial film-making?*

JVD: I'd like to make films the way other people play the piano or paint or write novels. I'd like it to be as light and free as that.

PH: *As solitary that.*

JVD: Not solitary. Having two or three companions is a lot less lonely than having eighty people in a crew. No, I'd just like the process to be more natural than the films I've made to date, which have been very hard, very awkward to shoot. There's another reason. When I write, I'm totally unfettered. I never think about production problems. I can decide, for instance, that I need a mouse to sing a song there and never worry about how I'm going to be able to achieve that effect.[1] I know I'll find a way. I write the

---

1 In *The Eighth Day*, in one scene, the 1950s pop star Luis Mariano appears as a mouse, scuttles under the floorboards and sings one of his songs in that disguise before turning back into a human again. Several Luis Mariano songs play a significant part in the screenplay.

film I want to see. That's all I think about. And now, I've started thinking that if I start shooting before I've started writing, then I'll discover a medium that's halfway between writing and cinema. Something more organic and natural so that writing and shooting won't be so distinct.

All this is partly a reaction against the awkwardness of dealing with so much money, but it's also that I want new subject-matter, I want to discover a new way of finding my subject-matter. The cumbersome thing about film-making is neither in the writing nor working with the actors. The actors get about twenty minutes a day. The rest is dealing with the technical crew, with infrastructure problems. The trick is to make your twenty minutes with the actors as pleasant and fruitful as possible. Camera position determines meaning and it has to be decided well in advance. There's something quite terrifying about long shoots designed to produce a careful continuum, a series of pre-determined meanings. *The Eighth Day* was an eighteen-week shoot. Every day had to generate a scene and every scene had to be right. The time available was predetermined and limited. Limited by the weather, the sun, by other organizational factors. And yet, you can't afford not to have a result. I'd like things to be different. I'd like the weather not to matter. I'd like to get good results not because everything has been planned to perfection, but because we've been able to chip away at a scene for as long as it takes.

PH: *This year, I subtitled a film by Alain Cavalier,*[1] La Rencontre, *which is an interesting case of someone who made big movies (by European standards), including a thriller with Alain Delon, and who is now working on his own, with just one friend and a Hi8 camera. He is able to obtain a commercial release for a film made like that.*

JVD: I've heard about it. I've had a similarly interesting experience: just after finishing shooting *The Eighth Day*, I was asked to use the first movie camera, the Lumière Brothers' camera. They were taking the camera round the world, asking film-makers everywhere to make one fifty-second shot. I'd just finished a major shoot and I saw a man get off the train here with a

---

1 Alain Cavalier: probably best known in Britain and America for his film *Thérèse*, a biography of a nineteenth-century French Catholic saint, entirely shot against a grey cylcorama.

satchel and no other equipment and he said, right, what are we doing? So I said let's put the camera here. And we looked at the sun and set up the tripod and asked Pascal to stand in front of it and he kissed his girlfriend and that was it. We used film-stock that was a facsimile of the original Lumière stock. The shot didn't look real. It looked like a representation of reality and that added a poetic dimension to the exercise. It was very straightforward. And that straightforwardness is part of the original function of cinema. All the technical sophistication that has intervened since has done nothing but make things seem complicated so they look more real. But most directors, and most cinematographers who use all this equipment (which is designed to reproduce reality as exactly as possible), spend their whole time trying to make the result seem less real, more poetic. Somewhere along the way, we've lost a lot of energy. But maybe if we can start doing things more simply we can recover some of that lost energy.

PH: *I have a feeling that there is some of that simplicity in the scene in which Pascal dances to Genesis in front of the TV screens, which you've said was almost improvised. And on the soundtrack, you've added a voice saying: 'This is a request from Jaco for Alice and Juliette.'*[1]

JVD: I used that song because Pascal loves it. When I put it on here, at home, he goes wild. I don't like it necessarily. But he does. Whereas he doesn't have any particular affinity for Luis Mariano.

I don't deliberately set out to combine industrial-scale film-making with more personal themes. Some of the critics implied I'd chosen to make a film about someone with a mental handicap because that was bound to appeal – as though I'd manipulated people's suffering in order to produce a hit. But I've never seen a Hollywood movie made with handicapped actors. There's no recipe for success. I make the films I want to see. I don't target particular audiences. I don't know anything about audience reactions, except what I get from a few friends who see the film while it's being made, or who read the script before we start shooting. They are people whose opinions I value and who give me feedback about what I've done. Those are the only views I

---

1 Alice and Juliette Van Dormael, Jaco's young daughters play the parts of Daniel Autueil's (Harry's) children in *The Eighth Day*. The film is also dedicated to them.

know. Whether the audience likes what I do or not is a question of chance. It does not enter into my calculations.

I am less involved in the financial aspect of film-making with a movie like *The Eighth Day* than with a short. PolyGram's involvement frees me from having to think about that. They came to me and said we'd like to produce your next film. So I said, I don't know, I have a feeling I'd like to make a film with mongoloid actors. A film about someone who meets a mongoloid character. Fine, they said, fine. As far as the script was concerned, the producer told me he'd like to see it, but it was entirely up to me. He said, do as you please, and take as long as you like over it. The only guidance he gave was that the movie should be beautiful. That kind of support meant I was much less involved in the business side of things.

PH: *But not worrying about money has aesthetic implications. When you say you write with a great deal of freedom, without considering the production consequences of what you're writing, that means you are going to encounter certain problems in the shooting which will be solved in a different way because you have a larger budget. The mouse is a good example. It would not have been made to sing in the same way if you'd had less money.*

JVD: Absolutely. In this instance, the effect is achieved by using computers. Every second of those special effects is extremely expensive. And the whole process is very arm's length. I get on the train to Paris. I call on a gentleman who sits at a computer and we discuss what the movement should look like. Two weeks later, I come back again and say the mouth should be a bit more . . . whatever. Two weeks later, I return and we take a look at the way the hips move. Two weeks later, I'm back and we think about the mouse's paws. All of this for a three-second shot. It's all very post-produced, very uninstantaneous. The pleasure is in the final result, not in the process. Computerized images somehow escape the director's control. He can give rough indications of what he wants but he doesn't sit with the technician typing numbers into a keyboard over a period of weeks.

PH: *What raw material did you provide?*

JVD: A mouse standing on its hind-legs, grabbing at a piece of cheese. We shot it on set to get the right background. We used a real mouse to get the right proportions.

xv

I didn't want the special effects to look like special effects. I wanted them to indicate a character's point of view, real or imaginary. I wanted them to look naïve. They belong to the characters' own worlds.

PH: *How was Luis Mariano on the bonnet of the car done?*

JVD: Back projection. We shot the background, then projected the footage behind the actor as he sat on the bonnet of a car. In real life, the actor in question looks vaguely like Luis Mariano, but he's wearing a false nose, false cheeks, hair implants, false eyebrows. He was coached both for singing and for posture. I told him what I wanted and he went off and studied with his coach for about a month and a half. They used tapes of Luis Mariano to get the shape of the lips right and so on.

PH: *I have a feeling that the range of music is wider in* The Eighth Day *than in* Toto.

JVD: The music was done by my brother in Dakar, in Africa, which is where he lives. He teaches at the Academy in Dakar and studies percussion in Senegal. He's a jazz musician, not a classical musician and he is convinced that jazz rhythms come from the traditional rhythms of a particular part of Senegal. That's his hobby-horse. The way we work is he sends me a set of musical ideas based on what he has read in the script and the screen tests he has seen. I rehearsed various scenes with Pascal before the shoot and shot them on video. I also recorded various improvisations of his. So my brother was able to view that material. Then he came up with various choices for the main themes and we sat down and selected the ones we wanted. Throughout the early stages of editing, I sent him a series of sequences and he'd send back bits of music. The next stage was more detailed. He came here, to Belgium, and we went through the cut saying we want such-and-such music here, such-and-such music here and so on. Then he sat down and rewrote the whole score, knowing what kind of music was going where. After that there was a final stage when he had to write the various different sections to length. The stringed instruments and some of the vocal music was recorded in Belgium. But the choral material was recorded in Africa, in Dakar. He also used some Australian aborigine instruments. He was interested in the contrast between African music and European symphonic music, to match the contrast between Georges and Harry in the film, so that at first the two were kept very separate, then gradually they were able to mingle. I wanted music that was extremely emotional because that is what I thought was needed for the kind of film I wanted to see. Some of the audience may reject the emotional charge of the music. At least that's what I sense in some of the criticism.

PH: *But then there is another kind of music in the film, like Luis Mariano's songs, which are a part of the script, as Charles Trenet's* Boum *was in* Toto. *Do you listen to Luis Mariano at home?*

JVD: No. (*Laughs.*) Well, once I did, yes. I listened to '*Maman, c'est toi la plus belle du monde*',[1] and '*Qui sait? qui sait?*' at my mother's house. One day, we gave her a record-player and she brought out her old 78s which we'd never heard. And when she put them on, I suddenly saw my mother as a twenty-year-old. Her eyes sparkled and so on. Speaking personally it's not really my cup of tea, but I can share . . . I mean, when I notice that my mother, whom I like, is moved and that she feels young again, I see there is something in it. It's out-of-date, old-fashioned, but it does have an emotional worth. And in the film, the music is associated with Georges' mother. The original idea was that every time he put on the song '*Maman, c'est toi la plus belle du monde*', his mother's ghost would appear. Then it grew into something else, and Luis Mariano appeared on the car bonnet and so on.

PH: *The mother was the first ghost, then you extended the idea so Harry's wife appears to him and Luis Mariano appears to Georges?*

JVD: Those dream sequences don't relate to reality but they do relate to the subject of the film, which is people's emotional journey. When Luis Mariano appears on the car bonnet, he is a visual expression of what Georges is feeling at that time. There is no narrative connection with what has come before, but there is an emotional continuity. Harry can't hear or see it. I wanted to make a film in which the main thread was emotional development and not dramatic construction. That's why those dream sequences work. They have no effect except in the immediate sense, they add nothing to the story.

PH: *When did you decide to cast your children?*

1 *Maman, c'est toi la plus belle du monde:* Mummy, you're the most beautiful woman in the world – the name of one of Luis Mariano's hits.

JVD: I wrote those parts for them because one of the hardest things about shooting is that you get cut off from the people you love. I try and work with people I like and love so I can go on seeing them.

PH: *But your children occupy a peculiar position in the script, since they are mistreated by their father. One wonders whether you are worried you might behave like that, or you feel guilty that you have done so. Once can't help thinking it's autobiographical.*

JVD: They don't see like that. They see it as acting. Actually, they reacted in totally different ways on set. The eldest would do thirty takes if I asked her to. The youngest couldn't give a damn. She'd say, I'll do it once, Dad, and that's it.

But to go back to the business of showing and provoking emotion – I have a feeling it's still something of a taboo. There's no taboo against violence, or sex now, but there is against emotion. Some people don't want to feel their emotions, they don't want to let go of themselves in a cinema. The film is strong meat for people like that. I don't usually read the critics till after the film is over and then I get sent a cuttings book 150 pages long. But this time I did see some of the articles and they were incredibly vehement. In France, the film did very well at the box office, but part of the press coverage was extremely hostile. And the first reactions we've had from Britain and from the States are very violent reactions against the film. They either say the film is too sentimental or they say I'm abusing handicapped people, as if they didn't know what they were doing, as if I could manipulate them by remote control and they didn't know they were acting.

PH: *There is one shot that worries me, which is the last shot of Daniel Auteuil (Harry) with the dustmen.*[1]

JVD: It's a fairy-tale ending. But there is a serious intention, which is to say I'm not interested in difference. Rather than saying we must tolerate difference, I'm saying we must not see difference, we must look beyond it. Most of us have a kind of primal fear of difference and I think that's what most of us feel when we see people with Down's syndrome. And that's a problem for them. I believe we've become degenerately social animals. We are incapable of living outside society. We can only feed ourselves and

1 In this shot, Harry, now parted from his handicapped friend, Georges, laughs and jokes with some African dustmen whom he helps load garbage into the truck.

clothe ourselves within our social group. If we withdraw from that
social group, we die. We can't live by hunting and gathering any
more. So I believe that we have acquired a kind of panicky, animal
mistrust for anything which does not conform to our social group
and might threaten it. This mistrust is very deep. It is also quite
unnecessary because we've reached a stage of social development
which means we can fit all kinds of differences into our social
system. But we put so much effort into matching the image we
have of ourselves with the image we have of other people, and that
effort is so very much at the top of the pyramid for us, that we
disparage everything which does not conform to it. But if we look
at the evolution of man, we see that, in the dinosaur age, our
ancestors were not the lordly dinosaurs but insignificant little
creatures of no status. Then circumstances changed and dinosaurs
disappeared. Continuity came in an unexpected way, from a lower
form of life. That's why the film argues that all forms of life are
equally valid. Georges treats all forms of animal and vegetable life
equally. And that's a point worth making because there's no way of
telling what form of life is going to enable life to carry on on earth.

PH: *Why does Georges kill himself?*[1]

JVD: As far as I'm concerned, he does not kill himself. He falls. He
devours a box of chocolates because he knows it's forbidden and
he wants to start doing as he pleases. He knows eating chocolates
is bad for him but he doesn't care, he wants the pleasure. He can't
help it. And for me . . . but perhaps there's something wrong with
the way I shot the scene, or I failed to shoot it . . . for me, he has a
kind of inspiration, connected with the song and the thought of his
mother. He comes to the edge of the roof and then, in his mind,
he flies away. And instead of flying, he falls. But the ending is
definitely a problem. For me he dies and it is not a suicide. But
even that was problematic. I wrote several different versions. I
read each one from beginning to end, with various different
endings. There was a happy ending in which he and Harry ended
up staying together. But that would have been a lie. That never
happens. If Harry had put him back in the asylum, that would

1 Near the end of the film, Georges obtains some chocolates, in the knowledge that
he is severely allergic to chocolate. He carries the chocolates up to the roof of a
skyscraper and consumes almost a whole box up there. Then he goes to the edge of
the roof and steps out over it.

have been terrifying. That would have been the saddest ending of all. So I chose an ending for the character that was less realistic, but which had the merit of making one miss the character. When I read that version, with that ending, I felt I wanted to see Georges again. The other endings seemed equally unrealistic, but at least this way an element of regret was brought in. And if the audience shares that regret, then the film has achieved something. If people come out of the cinema and meet a mongoloid on the bus, and they are pleased to see him, something has been won.

PH: *So it's like Arthur Conan Doyle, who killed off Sherlock Holmes and then had to bring him back by popular demand?*

JVD: If you think of them not as real characters but as fictional characters, then the ending is that Harry and George combine, they become the same person. Perhaps that's a bit of a conceit but if the film is a fairy-tale, then that's how the ending should be seen.

PH: *I have a feeling you are closer to the actors in this film than in* Toto. *I'm thinking of the fight between Miou-Miou (Julie) and Daniel Auteuil (Harry),*[1] *which is like the scene on the lawn outside the asylum in* Toto *in that it seems freer than the rest and more physical.*

JVD: Early on during shooting I realized just how cumbersome the whole process was going to be. I'd put all the easiest shots at the start of the schedule, but even they seemed to require an inordinate amount of technical work to achieve. So I extracted all the most important scenes from the schedule, most important from an acting point of view. And for those scenes, I asked the director of photography to give me 360° lighting and to use a hand-held camera, so we could work as fast as possible, with minimum technical constraint. I wanted to make sure that, for those scenes at least, technical considerations would be subordinate to the actors' needs. I told them that if the shots were out of focus, it wouldn't matter and we'd put them in the film out of focus. Consequently, we were able to do a hundred takes a day if necessary and really work at the energy, the intensity of those scenes. And of course those are the scenes I like best. There's

---

1 Harry and his wife Julie are living apart. Harry goes to his wife's house with a birthday present for one of his daughters, even though it is not yet his daughter's birthday. His wife's mother refuses to let him in, but he climbs in a window. His wife tries asking him to leave, and the scene turns into a fight.

Pascal at his sister's house, which is shot very close and the scene with Miou-Miou and Daniel. In that scene, Daniel had to get down on all fours and bark like a dog which was only going to work if we got it exactly right. And those scenes are crucial to the characters because they show them in another light. The disco was shot hand-held too. But those scenes are not improvised. They are in the script, dialogue and all. The difference is simply that, on the day, the actors were free to act in a completely different way. They had time to experiment.

PH: *And does that mean you had several possible versions by the time you got to the editing room?*

JVD: We shot 100,000 metres in all. It took us a week to view the rushes. But choosing the right shot was easy. There was always one take that was much better than the others.

PH: *I have a feeling that in each of your films, there's a part which is qualitatively different from the rest and that part is a foretaste of what are you going to do in your next film. In* The Eighth Day *it seems to me that the qualitatively different passages are the hand-held moments of brutality you've just referred to. Is that an indication of what are you going to tackle next?*

JVD: Those scenes were a pleasure to shoot. They're the heart of the film. Sometimes, in what I shoot, I'm trying for poetic effect, and then the shots rely on aesthetic choices about how we handle light and sound to help the audience see the film as a fairy-tale, even though the settings are very real, like cars and offices and police-stations. But these other scenes we're talking about work in a different way. They have to seem as tangible as possible. The impact is raw, so the aesthetics have to come second and the acting is what matters most.

PH: *Is the importance attached to acting in this film an inevitable product of the story, or is it related to the fact that you were able to work with a major French star who gave you more scope than other actors you've worked with, some of whom were non-professionals?*

JVD: I want to work closely with actors now. Apart from the fact that Daniel is so well-known in France, he is an actor who gives a great deal. He is not concerned with his image. He gave me as much as Pascal did. The pleasure that comes when you're working with actors is to have as much time and as much film stock as you need so you can try things out. The actors I work with tend to be a little put out in the first few days of working with me because I give contradictory directions. At first, they interpret this as a sign that I know exactly what I want and that I'm proposing different routes towards a specific goal. But it isn't like that. Sometimes, from one take to the next, I change my mind as to what we want to achieve, to see if we can't find something better and truer than what I had first intended. The psychology of the characters never alters, but their actions may.

PH: *Where do you stand during a take?*

JVD: Beside the camera. I check the start-frame and the end-frame in a monitor, otherwise I look at the actors. I don't give psychological notes. Which is just as well, because Daniel does not need them. He's an instinctive actor and I am an instinctive director. Pascal works on instinct too. The business of shooting a scene seems entirely empirical. None of the psychological indications one gives in advance can be right. They are always excuses for not being able to say the unsayable. Real motivation, whether of a character or of a film, is unsayable. The only way I know how to work is to give precise, empirical instructions about what to do and then correct those instructions according to instinct. Daniel and Pascal understand this. In fact, we didn't talk much.

PH: *Did you meet before the shoot?*

JVD: We had three days' rehearsal, but we ended up not bothering with formal rehearsals. The first day, Pascal had a tummy ache because he'd had too much to eat. The second day we went out. And the third day, I read out the script, very rapidly, skipping lots of scenes. The main thing was that we got to know each other. Something important was established between Pascal and Daniel. They laid the foundations.

PH: *Did you think they might not get on?*

JVD: I thought there might be days when they didn't get on. Because Pascal, like most actors with Down's syndrome, does as he pleases. He wants to have fun and if he doesn't the scene can go in the bin. He acts when he feels there's a pleasure there, a pleasure in pretending. For instance, when Pascal was doing a close-up, and Daniel was speaking to him from behind the camera, Daniel had to put as much feeling into the dialogue as if he'd been on camera, otherwise Pascal would have gone deaf. It would have been as if nothing had been said. It would have been just noise. With Down's syndrome sufferers, there has to be an emotional charge or nothing works. In other words, Pascal kept our standards very high. It had to be true, it had to be fun, we had to give it all we had. And I thought that might be very demanding for Daniel. Because Pascal is a bit up and down. He'll be good and then there'll be nothing there and then suddenly it'll be back with a vengeance. But you never know which it is going to be. There's no knowing if he's been distracted by a girl walking down the street, if he's hungry or got a tummy ache. So Daniel had to be at his best all the time. He had to be ready so that when Pascal switched on and was there, he had someone opposite him. But it really was very good.

PH: *Are they friends?*

JVD: Yes. I mean I'm the one who relates to both of them. For a long time it was me and Daniel and me and Pascal, then, slowly, they built a relationship. But if they see each other now, it's because I'm there. But I think Pascal was very good for Daniel because his demands were so high. Often, professional actors are nervous when they work with non-professionals. On *Toto*, Michel Bouquet was worried when he saw the non-professionals. He said, I'll look like an actor. They'll be true and I'll look like I'm pretending. I'll never manage to look as real as they do by working at it. Daniel was the same. But Pascal was acting too. In any case, Daniel's concern soon disappeared because you can't fake it when the other actor is like Pascal. If Daniel had faked it, the whole thing would have flopped.

PH: *After* Toto, *we discussed the kind of graphic formalism that using a storyboard can sometimes induce. Then, you told me storyboards were simply a convenience, an efficient way of communicating with the crew. I wondered whether your use of a storyboard had changed?*

JVD: My attitude to storyboards is slightly confused. Initially, on *The Eighth Day*, I'd decided not to use them. And before shooting, the only shots I storyboarded were the special effects scenes. I wanted to go out on set and see what would happen, to achieve something more organic and natural. But sometimes the fact that I kept having to explain exactly what I needed and that nobody really knew in advance what was going to happen caused a kind of lack of confidence. When eighty people have to prepare a shot and organize everything ahead of time, that kind of lack of confidence can create tension. The freedom I was asking for meant a lot more work for the crew. And sometimes, because of that, it cost us a great deal of time. The paradox is that you work without a storyboard in order to have more freedom, but because working without a storyboard makes greater demands on a crew, you end up feeling the technical pressures even more. So about one third of the way through the shoot, I started storyboarding the next day's shots the night before. I'd come on set in the morning and have more time with the actors.

I have no idea how I'll deal with this issue in the future. The thing is that when I write a scene, I see it very clearly, I see every shot and frame. I don't necessarily see it in the most interesting way, but at least I do see it. Whereas sometimes, when I go on set, I can be in a position where I no longer see the shot I'm looking for. The only thing I do know is that, as I was saying, the problem is not going to arise immediately because I want to start working at things that are not designed to be commercial, which I may not even finish, which are more experimental, more like some kind of diary. But, all the same, there is a great deal of pleasure to be had in creating very designed shots, prepared well in advance and discovering whether they work. There's a pleasure to be had in designing a house, then building it up and seeing if it turns out as expected.

PH: *Is there a connection between storyboarding and the Belgium tradition of strip cartoons?*[1] *Does the use of a storyboard facilitate a kind of humorous graphic design within the shots, the exaggeration of certain features, a face squashed against a pane of glass, an outsized white arrow in the road and so on?*

JVD: Cartoonists decide what they put inside the frame. We decide what to put outside it. We decide what not to include. The frame tells the audience what to look at. The relationship between different planes in a shot is a value judgement. The point of view shows who is telling a scene or who is living it and how it must be received. It indicates where the audience is situated within the story. Personally, I always try and make sure the audience is within the story, aligned with one or other of the characters. When

1 Tintin, for instance, is Belgian.

we define the frame, our freedom is the same as a writer's choosing his words.

Sometimes a frame is overdefined. It provides a simplistic language. This is a country without a shared language and that puts a lot of pressure on images. We use images as a language which all Belgians can understand, whether they are German-speaking or Flemish-speaking or French-speaking. Often, here, you'll see images which are ideograms, so people don't have to put a sign up in both the main languages. And when a sign is in both languages, separatists from one side will strike out the French word and then the other side will come and strike out the Flemish word and then no one can read the sign at all. There's an osmosis between my films and the country I live in.

PH: *But you didn't ask Auteuil to speak with a Belgian accent?*

JVD: Only when he says the word Bruxelles, pronouncing the x. We pronounce it 'Brusselles'. But there is something about Belgium. We have a kind of self-denigrating humour. The country is a kind of village. Now, with all our political problems, things have changed a bit, but I used to like making films here because it was like being nowhere. Like making films in a country that does not exist. We don't have the burden of French culture, all that good taste, Art with a capital A and Culture with a capital C. Here, we all disagree about everything, yet there is – or there was – a kind of consensus. We cohabit, but there's no dominant mood.

PH: *I have a feeling that the scene with the Indian in the turban would have been cut out of the script if it had been written in France. It might have been written on the spur of the moment, but it would have been cut out of a second draft.*

JVD: Actually that scene refers to an incident which happened to me. I took my wife and children to the house I grew up in in Germany and when I rang the doorbell, I was expecting a German lady to come out, but it was an Indian family that appeared, who spoke no German.

PH: *Did you grow up in Germany?*

JVD: Yes, my father worked for Seers, Roebuck in Frankfurt. He was a buyer. He never had to sell anything, he only bought, which was probably just as well. We lived in a village in the suburbs of Frankfurt. I went to a German school till I was seven. I still speak German like a seven-year-old. I can buy sweets in German, crucial things like that. I can't really talk about theory, or philosophy in German. But there too, the way they think is very different, just because the language is structured differently, the word order.

PH: *Do you ever want to make films anywhere else?*

JVD: I used to get a lot of screenplays from America. I'm very pleased that, in the end, I made this film here. But the only thing which determines where I make a film is the story. Some of the scripts I got from America were good, but I wasn't the right director for them. If the dialogue was too important, I didn't think I could manage in English. And for the others, I felt what I was writing would be better. Making a film means sacrificing, or giving, five years of one's life and as time is the most precious thing we've got . . . if it's someone else's script, it's still a year's preparation, a year's shooting and editing and a year to finish and sell the film. That's still three years. A film demands so much energy, whether one writes it oneself or not, you can only do it if you really feel, if I really feel that this film is essential. Otherwise, I'd be wasting my time and the audience's time. But if there was an essential film that had to be shot in Eskimoland, I'd go and shoot there.

PH: *Can we go back to how you might write the next film?*

JVD: I have no idea. I know that there's a part of me that enjoys constructing a story well. That's partly for the pleasure of making something well-designed and partly for another reason I'm trying to get rid of, which is that I tend to want to be invulnerable to criticism. A very well-crafted script in which all the bits of the puzzle hang together perfectly is invulnerable. No one can say a word against it. The structure can stop people asking whether a scene is good or not because it is necessary to the whole. But I'm beginning to think that's not necessarily a good thing. The script of *The Eighth Day* is much more vulnerable, in that sense, than the script of *Toto*. There are things in it people can be free to dislike because not all the scenes are essential to the structure.

PH: *Do you still read what you've written during the week to friends every Friday afternoon?*

JVD: For *The Eighth Day*, I'd meet two people I trusted about once a month and show them what I'd done. They'd ask me the right questions, which are always the simplest questions. Who is this character? Why is he doing such-and-such? And I did the same thing at various stages of editing. I asked friends, who are always the toughest critics because they know they're allowed to say whatever they please. I wanted to know if they saw the same thing I did. And there's always a great deal of difference between what I think is in a film and what other people see. I know that process is always going to matter.

But the fact that I'm alone at the computer has a considerable influence on my film-making, especially on the style. When there's a sudden shift in style midway through one of my films, that's because I've got bored at my desk. That's why, for instance, I suddenly want a mouse to break into song. After thinking of something like that, I feel refreshed, I can go on. If I didn't allow myself sudden changes like that, I'd have writer's block and probably change subject-matter. This way, I can go on finding different ways of saying the same thing. I usually reckon I'll cut my sudden inspirations out of the final draft, that they were there just to break the monotony. But often I keep them. The singing mouse is a case in point.

PH: *A lot of the things you go with, like the close-up of an ant being swept up into a vacuum cleaner, seem like Freudian pastiche.*

JVD: Someone wrote a thesis about the psychoanalytic interpretation of *Toto*. The title was sordid, something like 'Morbid compulsions in *Toto the Hero*'.

PH: *Can you say something more about why you keep all those close-ups of insects that fly away or fall into deep holes in the final cut? You had some in* Toto *too.*

JVD: To broaden the point of view. To show there are other worlds, other dimensions.

PH: *Buddhism?*

JVD: (*He laughs.*) In *The Eighth Day*, one of the main characters is blind to all the stories and all the universes which are not comprised in the image he sees every morning in the bathroom mirror, which are not comprised within the world he has made for himself. Then there's Georges, who is aware of all the possible ways of looking at the world. He knows that, if we could interview a mouse, the mouse would tell us the most important thing in the world is a piece of cheese. It would put itself at the pinnacle of the pyramid. Georges knows the mouse's world and our world coexist. A film always involves finding out about other worlds.

xxvii

None of our enquiries is exhaustive, but taken together they help something like the truth emerge. That's why people will always go on making films, because the only thing that matters is to carry on enquiring. Juxtaposing different worlds within a single story opens that story up. Otherwise, a story is funnel-shaped, tapered down to nothing at the end. Putting all those different worlds in a film is a way of saying this is what our story is about, but there are lots of other stories going on at the same time. The ladybird is not remotely interested in what is happening to Harry. Harry is not interested in the ladybird. Parallel worlds create a multiplicity. It's nice to be able to make even just visual connections between those worlds. And that's the point of the film. It's a film about two worlds which aren't ever supposed to meet. The film builds a bridge between them.

PH: *Putting close-ups of ants and ladybirds in a film implies a fairly languid sense of time. And yet the pace of your editing is very rapid. Sequences are put together with considerable narrative economy. Single shots contain all the information needed to move on to another sequence. You don't let us pause for long. Is the pace decided in the editing, or is it already implied in the way you write and shoot the scenes?*

JVD: It is decided at shooting script stage. It is very rare that I find a single angle that says everything I need to say. Probably, there are no such angles. An action may need to be shown in one way, but the next action will need to be seen from a different point of view because the mood has changed, the story has moved forwards, the relationship between the characters has changed. I can't usually connect two different points of view in a single shot because when I try to do that, when I try to move the camera from one place to another to link two shots, the rhythm slows down, and the sequence loses some of its intensity. Complicated shots also make technical difficulties, so the technical burden becomes even heavier. There is another reason. I'm always trying to talk about several different kinds of things at the same time. I like to establish contrasts. I like to jump from one mood to another and so on. But I have to say that I do try and be as fluid as I can. When I get into the cutting-room, I try and craft the whole so that the audience won't notice the jumps. I want the film to run as smoothly as possible.

In fact, my favourite shot is the one minute shot.[1] One whole minute's silence. It summarizes the whole film. I think so anyway.

PH: *There's another still shot like that, a wide landscape shot of a country road in storm light, where the filter is very obvious and you just stop the film so we can watch the light.*

But to hear you talk, it sounds slightly as though the film is already made when you get into the cutting-room. And I know that is not the case.

JVD: The first thing my editor, who has cut all my films since the early shorts, does is that she puts the film together as I have planned it. And that never works, so the real business of cutting begins. I always give myself enough cover to be able to alter things, to find the right subtleties of rhythm. The reason I enjoy the editing process so much is that I can forget all about the business of filming and go back to what I was thinking about when I wrote the script. Except that the script is written in words which are necessarily approximate. When I come to edit the film, I have to try and forget about the shots and retrieve the story. The picture edit takes about five or six months, and the sound edit comes after that. I was in a bit of hurry with *The Eighth Day*, so I delegated more of the sound edit than usual. I had several sound editors working at the same time and I used to move from one cutting-room to another.

PH: *Was the sound edit as complicated as with* Toto?

JVD: It was harder because the story does not take place in the imagination. There was a danger the sound might turn out very banal because the scenes are more realistic. We went for a more naked style, much more precise. At the same time, the sound had to be designed in such a way as to reinforce my idea that the film is a fairy-tale, which meant never quite being satisfied with natural sound. The sound of *Toto* was deliberately complex, full of conflicting sounds. With *The Eighth Day*, the idea was to create harmonies, to use different sounds that would build into something simple and interesting. For example, we'd use a normal city ambient sound, then add the same sound speeded up to give us a higher pitch, and the same sound slowed down to give us a

---

1 At one point, Georges and Harry lie in the grass at the foot of a tree. Harry says it's time to go. Georges says just a minute, and he times it. The shot is in a real time, and for one whole minute, the camera stays on Harry and Georges lying in the grass.

deeper harmonic and use the full range of different pitches, and then have the voices stand out against that background. The net result was just as rich but less convoluted than with *Toto*.

PH: *Have you ever wanted to make a film for children?*

JVD: Yes. My first short was for children. And I've written a children's book with Alice. But I'll certainly make a children's film before my kids are grown up. I've realized that half the films I see are children's films because I take my children to the cinema so often.

PH: *When we discussed* Toto, *you talked about how valuable Frank Daniel's[1] screenplay analysis had been and yet you said your favourite film was Tarkovsky's* Mirror *which hardly fits that mould. And now that you're saying you'd like to start shooting perhaps before sitting down to write a screenplay, I wonder whether your film-making is edging away from the highly structured style of* Toto?

JVD: But narrative structure is totally natural. The pleasure to be had in listening to a story is partly that we know the rules of the game, we recognize them. It's like football. If you don't know the rules, it seems pointless. But as soon as you know the rules, you can appreciate what is going on. Story-telling rules are an integral part of us, we know them naturally, whether we analyze them or not. They are as natural as walking. We have them in common. I remember telling you that Frank Daniel's favourite film was Fellini's *Amarcord*. He could analyze 40s American comedies down to the last detail, but when he watched *Amarcord*, he would be so involved in the story he would cry. His analysis of the structure of *Amarcord* was nevertheless identical to his analysis of American films. My children make up nursery rhymes and songs that have verses and choruses. They don't consider those rules a constraint because they naturally pertain to rhythmic structures. Stories naturally fall into three parts. You start off by saying, I am going to tell you a story, then you say now I'm telling you the story, and finally you say that was the story I was telling you. If you know what is going on, you can experiment with deliberate mistakes and see if that works, and know why it doesn't work if it doesn't work. You learn how to get round the rules.

PH: *There is a certain style of film-making which runs through* Toto

1 Frank Daniel, a well-known teacher of screenplay writing, who is Jaco Van Dormael's mentor. His influence is discussed in the interview pertaining more specifically to the making of *Toto the Hero*.

and The Eighth Day, *your sense of the graphic and so on. Do you think that is your style and that any film you make is bound to be in that style, or do you think you might embark on a film next year, or in two years' time in a completely different style?*

JVD: From the outside a film-maker's style probably always looks the same. But I'm inside the process and I know that I am not setting out to construct a body of work in a certain style. I want to escape my style. I want to do something I've never done before. I want to give myself up to the story and the characters. I want to deny myself. I tell myself this is not a film by Van Dormael. This is a film that doesn't have an *auteur*. The story belongs entirely to its characters. Every film is a new departure, with new characters. It has to stand on its own feet. I don't think the audience goes to the movies to see the next stage of an author's body of work. They go to see a single film, which lasts for two hours and is not connected to any other film. I think, quite naturally, a film-maker is most interested in subject-matter that is as far away from him or her as possible. The point is to tell a character's particular idiosyncratic truth. I don't have a sense that I must communicate what I know to be the case or what I think about life. The film is in the characters. I'm like an actor playing a part. Even when I'm writing. Writing is about trying to describe something which is very different to me, but which, inevitably, will throw up hidden parts of me. I never listen to Luis Mariano's music for instance. Georges' mother is the one who listens to Luis Mariano.

PH: *But Georges' mother has a connection with your mother.*

JVD: That's true.

PH: *I'm not sure I agree with what you were saying earlier. People do follow a body of work. They go and see a Marilyn Monroe movie or a Jean-Luc Godard movie, and that provides a kind of thread that runs through their life. Perhaps the most surprising thing in* The Eighth Day *are the scenes in which mongoloid characters suddenly appear in the middle of a steppe dressed as Oriental princes. It makes us laugh and yet it is unsettling and that is typical of Van Dormael's work. It may be what we're looking for when we go and see Jaco Van Dormael's latest film.*

JVD: My style may be that I am incapable of working in a single style. I have to use those stylistic mistakes to end up making films I enjoy. But the Mongolian scene is essential to the structure of the film. The word mongol had to be in the included, it had to come as soon as possible; Pascal's character, Georges, had to say it as soon as possible. The issue of that word, a name given to people, derived from a place those people have never been to and don't come from, that had to be dealt with. It's as though we were called Australians even though we'd never been to Australia. I wanted to give that word a connotation that was not pejorative. I wanted to say, these people are princes, they are Mongolian princes and princesses. They have a nobility. A lady told me that her son, who was mongoloid, had come home after seeing the movie, and he had always hated the word mongol, he'd never used it, and suddenly, when he saw the film, he started saying, with great pride, I'm a Mongol too, I'm a Mongol like those movie Mongols. He was proud of that. But it was very hard for Pascal to accept the word. When we started reading the script together, he'd pretend the word did not exist. Then when he got into it, he started using it with pride, he thought it was funny. And by the time we started shooting, he had lost his nervousness. But there had to be a stage where he could get over his initial reserve, over the sense that the word might be insulting.

PH: *What do they call themselves?*

JVD: The call themselves 'children' or 'people'. In the institutions they live in, they tend to be called 'young people' even when they are forty-five years old. On set, we used to call then *'les zozos'*, which they liked. It's a nice clown's name. They were proud to use that word themselves. But it's like black or negro. Words which signify difference easily sound insulting, but they can sound proud and respectful as well. I have a feeling that mentally handicapped people playing themselves in a movie, when before they would have been played by 'normal' actors, is a bit like what happened the first time black actors played black people in films. In the days of silent movies, black characters were played by blacked-up white actors because it did not occur to people that black people were capable of acting. But as soon as the taboo was lifted the absurdity of it became apparent. And it's the same here. Down's syndrome sufferers are very good actors.

PH: *Did the actress who plays Nathalie[1] know how to ride before the shoot?*

1 Georges is in love with a fellow patient called Nathalie whose parents are wealthy. She leaves the asylum and is discovered later riding horseback.

JVD: No, she didn't. But there are people with Down's syndrome of all classes and they preserve the distinctive traits of their backgrounds, much more than we do because we've all been homogenized by education. We've been taught to play up our similarity to other people, to emphasize our belonging to the tribe. I feel their characters, their personal traits are very varied. Pascal is a very good actor. Some don't know how to act at all. Some are good at painting. Some are very good at eating and nothing else. One of the people who looked after them used to say, 'They're slightly crazy, but you have to be slightly crazy otherwise you go mad.' And that's it. Harry goes mad. The parents I know who have children with Down's syndrome are amazing. There is something transcendent about them. I mean, either it breaks them or they become really remarkable people. The hard thing is that inevitably they stand between their children and the rest of the world. Their children cannot become functional cogs in society. And that's very uncomfortable. The parents feel their children are rejected but often that feeling frees something in them. They learn to see things as they are, without prejudice. Often they say, he or she is the best thing that happened to us. It's the worst thing that happened to us, but it's also the best thing that happened to us. People with Down's syndrome demand an enormous amount of affection but they give a great deal in return.

PH: *And it's the same with you isn't it? First you try and make a documentary about them and they take over, then you make a short film using them as actors, then they have a small part in* Toto, *and now they are at the centre of your new film. In a way, you are in the same situation as their parents. You stand between them and the world, you give them a great deal and they give you a great deal in return.*

JVD: Yes. It's as if I'd discovered a new country or a continent that's so close to home you only have to turn your head to see it. I only want to show other people what I think I've discovered. And though it's so close, we try and ignore it. They don't appear in films because they don't appear in our lives. If they did appear in our lives, they'd be part of our imaginative worlds. Instead of which they are kept in the cellar, or outside. Despite their power, despite what they can do for the way we see the world. They are free spirits. We have gained a lot by abandoning the mongol within us, but we have lost a lot too. We have gained the right to be in the world.

PH: *You say this in the film, but it's as though you didn't want it to be too heavy, as though you reverted to a comic mode to be able to get this message through without too much pain. I'm thinking of that very graphic shot of Georges' sister waving goodbye, seen through the back window of Harry's car, which is like a comic-book goodbye, after a very demanding and naturalistically portrayed family crisis.*

JVD: I don't think of that shot as comic. I think of it as poetic, a poignant moment because Georges may never see his sister again. But it's true that I like to use laughter. Laughter enables one to talk about everything, to create a great deal of tension, then to remove it. When I go to the movies, I like to feel good at the end, even though the film may have been about important and difficult subjects. I don't want to go home burdened with anxiety. In Hitchcock's films, the tension and anxiety are always resolved in the end. Unlike today's films in which you leave the theatre wanting to install a new alarm system in your house. I need to feel some kind of reconciliation with my fellow humans, and with life in general, at the end of a movie.

PH: *And why do you use so much music?*

JVD: To remind people it's just a film. Singing and dancing transports the story away from humdrum reality.

PH: *Is there a fraternity of other film-makers, whom you feel close to in this respect?*

JVD: I feel close to people who make films that I couldn't make. Ken Loach, for instance. *Raining Stones* is a prodigious film, so light and true. Maybe Terry Gilliam too, for his style. His subject-matter tends to be serious, but he treats it in a light-hearted way. Anything goes. He's very imaginative.

PH: *I'd like to find a way of talking about the future in a little more detail, but I sense that is not something you really feel like talking about.*

JVD: I've finished *The Eighth Day*. I'm waiting for a story to grab me, like a virus. I need to feel it in my bones, to be feverish. I need not to be able to live without it. Then I'll make that film and it will be as if it was the only film in the world. And then I'll do nothing again. When a film ends, life starts up again. When I'm shooting, time passes so fast, I'm inside the fiction, I'm not living my life. I need a gap between films to come back to the land of the living, so

I can breathe, and generate new fiction.

I enjoy talking like this because the normal thing that happens when you go out and promote a film is of a different order. People treat you like a fictional character. You arrive somewhere and people think they know you. They know nothing about you, but when they talk to you they give you the impression that they do. I always feel they are speaking to someone other than me, someone standing behind me. There's a strange discrepancy between normal life and the life of a film-maker. That's why it's so important to hang on to your normal life. After *The Eighth Day*, people came up and hugged me, which was pleasant, but there were others who came and insulted me, and then vanished. I'd never seen them before and I'll never see them again. They've got this notion of who I am based on the experience of seeing the film.

PH: *Is that because of the nature of* The Eighth Day?

JVD: No. I think it's going to happen more and more. Right now, I feel like I have been beaten up.

PH: *Is that why you'd like to make simpler, more private films?*

JVD: Not at all. That's to do with the technical burden of making a large film and what it takes in terms of human energy. Even if you take a few knocks, you can only go on doing what you believe in. Sometimes I'm lucky because audiences will react the way I do, and sometimes I'll be less lucky because they'll react differently. But I can't change. People are entitled to disagree. But there's something else. If a film takes up five years of my life, that's one thing. But you also have to think of the number of man-hours involved in audiences watching a movie. It's probably about two or three thousand years of human life. And I'm the only judge of whether I'm using that amount of time responsibly. If I try and compromise with other people's opinions, then those thousands of years of human life spent watching my film are bound to be wasted. The only thing a film-maker can do is to believe in what he does.

PH: *But would you have said the same thing four or five years ago?*

JVD: I think so.

PH: *So what difference has the anger provoked by* The Eighth Day *made?*

JVD: The worst thing I can do is to protect myself. I think I can avoid that. I have to let myself endure people's negative reactions, and enjoy their positive reactions. Sounds a bit pompous, doesn't it?

But I think I made myself more vulnerable over *The Eighth Day* than over *Toto the Hero*, because the dramatic structure is voluntarily flawed. It allows all kinds of emotional reactions.

PH: *Any particular sequences?*

JVD: The girl dancing in the disco, the minute's silence, the moments when Georges and Harry give each other a big hug. Those things can irritate people because they are outside the dramatic structure. They are probably the best things I can do, but in doing them I'm lowering my guard and I shall have to go on lowering my guard. Because if I were to make tighter, better crafted, buckled-down, sophisticated, unshakeable, unexceptional films, then I'd be avoiding the issue; I'd be less generous.

PH: *Surely people are not aware that the dramatic structure gives them scope to be irritated. They think they are taking the initiative in reacting to your use of an actor with Down's syndrome.*

JVD: Yes. But I didn't expect the problem to arise in the way it did. I didn't expect the critics to react so violently. I thought the general public might have trouble identifying with Pascal. But that has not proved to be the case. I believe there was a need for audiences to see someone like him acting in a film. I had that need and I believe audiences had it too. And I'm glad I was right about that.

The Eighth Day

The Eighth Day was first shown at the 1996 Cannes Film Festival.
The cast and crew include:

HARRY	Daniel Auteuil
GEORGES	Pascal Duquenne
JULIE	Miou-Miou
GEORGES' MOTHER	Isabelle Sadoyan
COMPANY DIRECTOR	Henri Garcin
NATHALIE	Michele Maes
LUIS MARIANO	Laslo Harmati
JULIE'S MOTHER	Helene Roussel
FABIENNE	Fabienne Loriaux
FABIENNE'S HUSBAND	Didier de Neck
ALICE	Alice Van Dormael
JULIETTE	Juliette Van Dormael
Director of Photography	Walther Van den Ende
Set Design	Hubert Pouille
Costumes	Yan Tax
Editor	Susana Rossberg
Sound Editor	Philippe Bourgeuil
Original Score	Pierre Van Dormael
Screenplay and Dialogue	Jaco Van Dormael
Screenplay Consultants	Laurette Vankeerberghen
	Didier de Neck
Line Producers	Eric Rommeluere
	Dominique Josset
Producer	Philippe Godeau
Director	Jaco Van Dormael

A Pan-European Production
Released in the United Kingdom and the United States by
Polygram

VARIOUS

Fade in. The perforations of an old film wipe across the screen. No image.

GEORGES
(*voice-over*)

In the beginning, there was nothing, nothing at all. Just music.

Luis Mariano's voice sounds in the distance. Visual buzz of a television screen. An image appears: Luis Mariano surrounded by dancers.

LUIS MARIANO
(*singing*)

Mexico . . . Mexiiiiico . . . Sous ton soleil
qui chante-hii-le temps paraît trop court
pour goûter au bonheur de chaque jour . . .[1]

EXT. SUN AND INSTITUTE GROUNDS. DAY

Dazzling sun in the sky.

GEORGES
(*voice-over*)

On the first day, he made the sun. He switched on the day and switched out the night . . . Everyone's eyes started to sting. Then he made the earth . . .

Gradually, we descend beneath the sun, a layer of white cotton cloud . . . through the cloud, which darkens . . . Thunder . . . Black cloud . . . It's raining cats and dogs . . . A flash of lightning. Further down, the branches of a tree . . . A swing in the grounds of some sort of institution. On the swing, from behind, a grown man, silhouetted and soaking wet. This is Georges, who sways gently in a plastic mac, with the hood on. Rain pours down on him.

1 Mexico . . . Mexiiiiico . . . Beneath your melodious sun
time flies and everyday happiness just slips by . . .

Drops trickle over his hand, into his palm and up his wrist.

Water's wet. It makes you cold.

Clouds reflected in a puddle. The water stops.

The top of Georges's head. His hair ruffled in the wind. He strokes his hair.

Wind tickles.

A lawnmower passes by. The blades squeal. Georges's hand caresses the grass.

On the second day, he made grass. When you cut it, it screams because it hurts. You have to make it better by saying something nice. Cows eat grass. I like cows. They blow warm.

EXT. FIELD. DAY

Georges's hand strokes a cow's moist nose.

INT. ROOM IN THE INSTITUTE. NIGHT

A map of the earth, misshapen, all out of proportion, surrounded by brushes and paints. We come closer . . . and discover the names of countries we don't exactly recognize: 'Africa', 'West', 'Sea', 'Mongolia' . . .

GEORGES
(*voice-over*)

Then he put countries on earth. He called the country full of water 'The Sea'. It's wet. Your feet get wet when you walk in it.

EXT. SEA. DAY

From above, a pair of shoes on the sand. A wave slips across the sand and floods the shoes.

INT. LIVING-ROOM, INSTITUTE. DAY

Television programme: a Japanese musician wearing a tail-coat.

GEORGES
(*voice-over*)

On the third day, he put people in the countries. They come in all different colours. Yellow, black, white, red. But not green. Green's not allowed.

INT. ROOM IN THE INSTITUTE. DAY

A record placed by Georges on a turntable.

RECORD
(*language lesson: English*)

'My table is yellow . . . This is John . . . John and Mary are married.'

In Georges's hand, a model of a newly-wed couple, such as might go on a wedding cake.

GEORGES
(*voice-over; repeating*)

. . . 'This is John. John and Mary are married.' People born in America speak English. What they say is hard to understand. I don't remember where I was born, I was too small. I think it was in Mongolia.

EXT. MONGOLIA. DAY

Gusting wind. The immense majesty of the Mongolian steppe. Grass as far as the eye can see, swaying in the wind. A horse gallops in the distance. A Mongolian baby in swaddling clothes on the grass, crying.

INT. LIVING-ROOM. DAY

Television image: a map of Mongolia. In on the word 'Mongolia'. The smiling face of a Mongol on horseback beside a yurt. He waves at the camera. His eyes are slit.

Georges watching television. He suffers from Down's syndrome. His hand meticulously imitates the gestures of the man on television but there is a slight delay. His fingers touch the remote control. A cookery programme. The chef pours chocolate sauce over some cakes. Georges imitates the chef's gestures. Then zaps over. A pair of comedians.

*Georges imitates what they do. Then zaps over. An animal programme.
A herd of reindeer, a shoal of fish, a herd of zebra . . . a lame zebra,
apart from the rest, is attacked by a lioness.*

> GEORGES
> (*voice-over*)
> On the fourth day, he made TVs and put people inside them.
> He made chocolate, but chocolate is bad. He made elephants,
> zebras, mice, shellfish, macaroni, ants and trees.

EXT. INSTITUTE GROUNDS. DAY

Georges strokes a tree trunk, then hugs it.

> GEORGES
> (*voice-over*)
> If you touch a tree, you become a tree.

We move up the bark . . . along the branches, into the leaves . . .

Georges, lying on the grass, closes his eyes.

> If you close your eyes, you can be an ant.

INT. LIVING-ROOM, INSTITUTE. DAY

*In the living-room, an ant edges on to the carpet. A vacuum-cleaner
brush moves in and swallows the ant. The ant is propelled through the
vacuum-cleaner tubes and vanishes into a black hole. A scream.*

EXT. INSTITUTE GROUNDS. DAY

Georges opens his eyes and screams. He catches his breath.

*Other patients move across the lawns: Jean, Jacques, Dominique,
Alain, Fernand . . .*

> GEORGES
> (*voice-over*)
> On the fifth day, he made men and women. Jean, Guy,
> Jacques, Fernand, Pierre are men.

INT. CORRIDOR AND BALLROOM, INSTITUTE. DAY

Georges edges the door open and looks through the crack. In the ballroom, he sees Nathalie, a Down's syndrome sufferer the same age as he is. She is dressed in a tutu, dancing. She seems lovely and graceful. Georges is open-mouthed.

> GEORGES
> (*voice-over*)
> Nathalie is a woman. I prefer women, because they don't prickle when you kiss them. Later Nathalie and I are going to get married, except we can't.

INT. CORRIDOR, INSTITUTE. DAY

Georges rests his head on Nathalie's shoulder.

> NATHALIE
> No way. I'm in love with Johnny Halliday.

INT. PHOTOGRAPHER'S STUDIO. DAY

A couple of models dressed as newly-weds pose for the camera. The Photographer tells them to squeeze up close.

> GEORGES
> (*voice-over*)
> To have a baby, a man and woman look at each other. They don't know each other. So they swap names and then they get married.

> PHOTOGRAPHER
> (*off-screen*)
> Try and look a bit more confident.

The models don't understand.

> MALE MODEL
> Confident about what?

> PHOTOGRAPHER
> (*irritated*)
> About the future!

The couple adopt a vaguely confident air. The flash goes off.

EXT. ROAD. DAY

The photograph with the models is now a poster by the side of a road. The poster carries a slogan: DELTA BANK. A BANK THAT CARES ABOUT YOUR FUTURE.

> GEORGES
> (*voice-over*)
> They marry and kiss each other on the mouth, the way they do on television.

TELEVISION

On TV, an old movie. Luis Mariano kisses a girl.

> GEORGES
> (*voice-over*)
> They hug each other for about half an hour and then a tiny seed starts growing.

EXT. FIELD. DAY

A combine harvester. Grain sprays out of a hose.

> GEORGES
> (*voice-over*)
> Only one seed makes it all the way. It's like a race.

EXT. MONGOLIA. DAY

The baby in swaddling clothes cries on the grass.

> GEORGES
> (*voice-over*)
> Then a baby gets born under a rock or in a bra. He has to drink breast-milk to get big and strong.

A hand lifts up a rock. Ants scatter.

INT. MATERNITY WARD. DAY

A woman in a dressing-gown (Georges's mother), in tears, sitting on a bed with her head in her hands.

> **GEORGES**
> (*voice-over*)
> And everyone's happy. If it's a boy, they call it Georges.

INT. ROOM IN THE INSTITUTE. DAY

Georges's reflection in the mirror. He ties a knot in his tie. His hair is immaculately combed.

> **GEORGES**
> (*voice-over*)
> So the baby has to become a grown-up, which means getting up and getting dressed all by himself. He has to look nice so he can find himself a wife later on and get married.

INT. VARIOUS. DAY

A bar of soap. A tie being done up. A plate, a knife, a fork. A green light. Shake of hands.

> **GEORGES**
> (*voice-over*)
> Wash with soap. Put on a nice tie. Knife on the right, fork on the left. *Bon appétit.* Eat properly. Do as you're told. Say thank you. Kissing people with your tongue is not nice. Not nice at all. Now give your teeth a good brush.

INT. LIVING-ROOM, INSTITUTE. DAY

Georges watching TV. A commercial. A man brushing his teeth. Georges imitates his gestures. The man grabs a tube of toothpaste.

> **MAN**
> Everyday, I use DENTEX. DENTEX strengthens . . .

Someone passes by and lowers the sound on the TV. The commercial continues. Georges's voice is perfectly in sync with the actor's lips.

. . . the enamel on my teeth and keeps my gums healthy.
DENTEX for dental hygiene.

INT. ROOM IN THE INSTITUTE. NIGHT

Georges's fingers count to six.

He opens a cupboard filled with a strange variety of objects. He rolls a miniature car beside a model house belonging to a toy train set.

GEORGES
(*voice-over*)
On the sixth day, he made everything he'd forgotten up till then: houses, records, radios, fridges, cars . . .

Georges lies on his bed. Jean and Jacques sit beside him. There is no light. Jean whispers an explanation to Georges.

JEAN
Cars come in big sizes and small, red, blue and green. Oh yes, green too.

JACQUES
And yellow.

INT. CORRIDORS, INSTITUTE. DAY

GEORGES
(*voice-over*)
He put arrows everywhere so we'd know which way to go.

A corridor. An arrow points the way. Georges shows the direction of the arrow.

EXT. INSTITUTE GROUNDS. DAY

Georges on a swing. He is skilfully knitting a woollen scarf. He looks up. Great swirls of cloud ease across the sky.

GEORGES
(*voice-over*)
Sunday, he had a rest. It was the seventh day.

Georges lies on the grass. The sun is shining. He watches a ladybird clambering up a blade of grass.

Georges closes his eyes. The ladybird spreads its wings and flies away. Georges concentrates. He spreads his arms. A gust of wind ruffles his hair. The camera flies off way above Georges. We pass over the swing, the trees, the roofs. Georges is a dot on the lawn.

EXT. SKY. DAY

Higher still. The houses look tiny. Swirls of cloud pass between us and the earth.

We climb above the clouds. A white mattress as far as the eye can see. Music.

A title: THE EIGHTH DAY.

The title fades. A plane flies past, very close, with a deafening burst of wind, and dives full blast into the landscape.

INT. PLANE. DAY

On board a plane, businessmen reading or dozing. They all look roughly the same. Among them, Harry, about forty.

> AIR HOSTESS'S VOICE
> Please extinguish all cigarettes and fasten your seat-belts. Kindly remain seated until the plane comes to a complete stop. You will find your luggage inside the terminal building, carousel B.

INT. AIRPORT. DAY

Harry on a moving walkway, surrounded by other businessmen dressed in the same style. He seems uneasy. Arrows. The walkway moves inexorably but not fast.

> AIR HOSTESS'S VOICE
> Passengers with goods to declare are requested to follow the red signs. If you have nothing to declare, please follow the green signs.

Suitcases land on the carousel in the baggage hall. We follow one suitcase, which Harry lifts off the carousel.

EXT. CITY. NIGHT

A boulevard. Harry at the wheel of his car. He pauses at a red light. A tramp comes towards him. Harry looks away. The tramp knocks at the window. Harry looks uneasily ahead. The light turns to green. He moves off.

INT. HARRY'S LIVING-ROOM/CHILDREN'S ROOM. NIGHT

Through the open door, we see Harry enter the large, empty living area and put down his suitcase. He presses the button on the answering-machine.

JULIE'S VOICE

Harry? It's me – The girls haven't seen you for months . . . They'd be very disappointed if . . . *Biip.*

ALICE'S VOICE

Daddy? Mummy says can you come and pick us up on Friday? She doesn't know how to drive us because her car is broken. *Biip.*

Harry switches off the answering-machine. He moves forward and enters the children's room. He does not turn the light on. He sits on the bed and examines the darkened room. A few toys, a photograph of two children. Harry glances at the cupboard, which is open. All the hangers are empty. There is one pair of abandoned children's shoes.

INT. HARRY'S BEDROOM. DAY

The alarm clock moves to 7.30. The radio comes on.

PRESENTER'S VOICE

It is 7.30 a.m. and the outside temperature is . . . *(continues)*

INT. HARRY'S KITCHEN. DAY

A slice of toast jumps out of the toaster.

INT. HARRY'S BATHROOM. DAY

The toothbrush drops back into its glass. Harry smiles at his reflection.

EXT. HARRY'S STREET. DAY

The automatic door of the garage opens. Harry's car emerges. His house is a prosperous-looking and unremarkable villa in a residential neighbourhood. The door closes. A refuse truck passes by, picking up rubbish.

EXT. MOTORWAY. DAY

Harry drives down the motorway in a sea of cars. He shaves as he drives. Parallel lines on the road. Numbered arrows. Silhouetted drivers in other cars, making telephone calls from behind their steering wheels. We fly above the motorway full of cars. Harry uses a phone mike so he can talk without using his hands.

BRUNO
(off-screen; telephone)

We're meeting the Weston people at 11.30, then it's the General at 11.45.

HARRY

Reschedule. Give the Weston people thirty minutes. They're the big one.

BRUNO
(off-screen)

And there's a message from your wife about . . .

HARRY

I know. I don't have time to pick them up. I don't care how you do it, but you've got to persuade her to put the kids on the train. I'll get them from the station. Tell her I swear I'll be at the station.

EXT. CITY STREET. DAY

A traffic jam. Harry's car is stuck. A refuse truck blocks the way ahead. The refuse collectors are picking up bins. Harry checks his watch. He

*loses his temper and starts honking. One of the men turns round and
gives him the finger.*

GEORGES
(*voice-over*)

People work to earn money. Animals don't work. They do as
they please. Which is why they get eaten.

EXT. PASTURE. DAY

A cow in a field.

GEORGES
(*voice-over*)

Cows get eaten even if they are nice. I used to know one
called Catherine. The people at the supermarket ate her, I
think.

INT. SUPERMARKET. DAY

*A polystyrene tray of plastic-wrapped meat on a stand. A hand with
red-varnished nails takes the tray and digs its thumb into the meat.*

INT. MEETING-ROOM. DAY

*A committee gathered about an oval-shaped table in a large meeting-
room. Harry stands beside the Director. Clients, across from him, listen
as he speaks. Bruno, a young man, hands him documents. The 'Delta
Bank' poster is behind them.*

HARRY

A new image. That's what we're going to create. A new image
for your bank. A more human image. Eighty per cent of your
customers' decisions are based on their emotional reactions,
their first impressions, their intuition. They are not logical.

*He shows the poster: newly-weds, smiling. Harry moves around the
table.*

The campaign plays to this. Everyone wants to be loved.
You're selling love. Not bank accounts. But don't forget, your
image is your employees' image. How they behave towards
the client. How they talk to them. What they wear. How they

look. How they smile. Nothing can be left to chance. Our job is to act as consultants to businesses and to train staff. We do not take decisions. They are your decisions. Think it over . . . A new image.

He sits down. Everyone looks at the older man. He pauses for reflection. No one speaks. Then he rises and shakes Harry's hand.

> CLIENT
>
> Thank you . . . we're giving you a green light.

Everyone talks at once. Applause, congratulations. The Director stands.

> DIRECTOR
>
> Your annual general meeting is on 15 May. That doesn't give us much time.

Everyone stands. Harry makes his way to the door, shaking hands as he goes. He comes across the Director and the Client.

> CLIENT
>
> We need something spectacular for the annual general meeting . . . a firework display maybe.

> DIRECTOR
>
> Why not? Great idea.

Harry vanishes.

INT. HARRY'S OFFICE. DAY

Harry sits at his desk without moving. The Director opens the door. He is surprised to see Harry there. Noise and laughter from outside.

> DIRECTOR
>
> So there you are. We've been looking for you everywhere.

He shuts the door and sits on the desk.

Is anything wrong?

> HARRY
>
> No . . . I'm fine . . .

> DIRECTOR
>
> You're not sick, I hope? They're all waiting for you.

17

HARRY

I . . . I needed to be alone . . . I'm not . . .

DIRECTOR

Not what?

HARRY

Not sure . . .

DIRECTOR

About what?

HARRY

I don't know. I am thinking.

DIRECTOR

What about?

HARRY

About . . . life.

The Director is puzzled.

DIRECTOR

Ah. About life.

They fall silent.

INT. LARGE ROOM. DAY

A group of employees take notes as Harry speaks.

HARRY

This method concerns you all because we're all salesmen. Every one of us, at one time or another, sells a part of himself. So obey the four cardinal rules. One: LOOK your client in the eye. Two: SMILE. Three: show that you're SUCCESSFUL – people prefer to deal with successful people. People who are past it put them off. Four: Be ENTHUSIASTIC. Enthusiasm is contagious.

INT. OFFICE TOILETS. DAY

Harry leans on a washbasin. He slaps water on to his face. He feels sick. He stares at himself in the mirror. Slowly, he breaks into a smile. Then the smile collapses.

INT. HARRY'S BEDROOM. DAY

The alarm clock moves to 7.30. The radio comes on.

PRESENTER'S VOICE
It is 7.30 a.m. and the outside temperature is . . . (*continues*)

INT. HARRY'S KITCHEN. DAY

A slice of toast jumps out of the toaster.

INT. HARRY'S BATHROOM. DAY

The toothbrush drops back into the glass. Harry smiles at his reflection.

HARRY
(*off-screen*)
Be filled with an unshakeable conviction that you are a
winner. Think positive . . .

EXT. HARRY'S STREET. DAY

The automatic door of the garage opens. Harry's car emerges.

HARRY
(*off-screen*)
Only use positive words. Throw negative words right out of
your vocabulary.

INT. LARGE ROOM. DAY

The same employees take notes as Harry speaks.

HARRY
Be proud of yourselves. Of course, that doesn't mean you
have to smile at yourself in the mirror every morning.
(*Laughter.*) Just be proud of yourselves. And of Delta Bank.

EXT. HARRY'S STREET. NIGHT

*The garage door opens automatically. Harry's car enters. The door
closes.*

INT. HARRY'S BEDROOM. DAY

The alarm clock moves to 7.30. The radio comes on.

> PRESENTER'S VOICE
> It is 7.30 a.m. and the outside temperature is . . . (*continues*)

INT. HARRY'S KITCHEN. DAY

A slice of toast jumps out of the toaster.

INT. HARRY'S BATHROOM. DAY

The toothbrush drops back into its glass. Harry smiles at his reflection.

EXT. HARRY'S STREET. DAY

The automatic door of the garage opens. Harry's car emerges.

> HARRY
> (*off-screen*)
> Try and be like your customer . . .

INT. LARGE ROOM. DAY

Harry strolls up and down between the employees as they listen to him.

> HARRY
> Watch him. Copy his gestures, his attitudes, his intonations. Two like individuals are more likely to be on the same wavelength than two people who are different.

He pauses beside one of the employees and mimics his posture. Laughter.

> The other person will never notice you are imitating them, I promise. People don't notice similarity. They only notice difference and they don't like it.

EXT. STATION. EVENING

A train pulls into the station. Two children get off, Alice and Juliette, aged seven and four. The older girl holds her younger sister by the hand. They look around. The crowd on the platform dispels.

INT. LARGE ROOM. EVENING

The room empties. The Director comes in. He needs to speak to Harry.

DIRECTOR

Have you got a minute, Harry? You're not seeing any of our customers this evening, are you?

Harry sits down.

We need the President's speech by Tuesday. The annual general meeting's been moved forward a day, to the 14th.

Harry checks his diary.

HARRY

The 14th? Damn, that's my daughter's birthday.

DIRECTOR

To tell you the truth, it's my wife's birthday. There's nothing we can do about it.

Suddenly, Harry realizes.

HARRY

The girls!

EXT. STATION. NIGHT

The two children are on a bench. Night has fallen. The station is deserted. They wait. Alice takes Juliette by the hand and goes to check departure times on a board which is difficult for her to decipher.

EXT. CITY STREET. NIGHT

Harry runs as fast as he can.

EXT. STATION. NIGHT

Alice and Juliette get on a train. The doors shut. The train leaves.

EXT. STATION. NIGHT

Harry appears in the station. The platform is empty.

INT. HARRY'S GARAGE. NIGHT

The car enters the garage. The garage door closes automatically. Harry gets out of the car and pauses for a moment in the dark. The car door remains open.

SYNTHESIZED VOICE
Your door is open . . . Your door is open . . .

Irritated, he slams the door closed.

INT. HARRY'S SITTING-ROOM. NIGHT

Harry is in an armchair. The telephone is right in front of him. He seems exhausted. He leans forward. He's caught sight of something beneath an armchair. He gets down on all fours and slides his hand in. He finds a child's sock. He examines it. He is moved.

The telephone rings. Harry rushes to get it.

HARRY
Hello?

JULIE'S VOICE
It's Julie.

Pause.

The girls are home.

HARRY
How are they?

JULIE'S VOICE
They're fine. They don't want to see you, though.

HARRY
What?

JULIE'S VOICE
I think you shouldn't try to see them for a while. I think that's probably best, for them.

HARRY
Let me have a word with Alice.

Harry, she doesn't want to.

Pause.

                    HARRY
I'm coming over. I have to talk to them. I'll be right over.

                 JULIE'S VOICE
No. Don't. We have an agreement. You don't come here.

She hangs up.

INT. GEORGES'S ROOM. DAY

Georges is packing. He gathers up a few clothes, his records, some treasures, a biscuit tin . . . his stuff.

EXT. INSTITUTE GROUNDS. DAY

Cars park in the grounds. Relatives – most of them elderly – load up bags into the boots of their cars. Laughter, happiness, goodbyes. Nathalie gets into her parents' car.

Georges appears on the steps, immaculately combed. He is carrying a suitcase and he has put on his best suit. One of his friends passes nearby.

                  DOMINIQUE
Have a nice weekend.

One of the staff sees Georges.

                 STAFF MEMBER
Georges! What are you doing?

                    GEORGES
My mum's coming, to fetch Georges.

The Staff Member looks slightly sorry for Georges and puts a hand on his shoulder.

                 STAFF MEMBER
Come on, Georges. Go put your stuff away. Guess what?
We've got French fries this evening.

I hate French fries.

Georges does not move. He seems sad, watching the cars drive off.

The grounds are empty now. There's no one around. A dog approaches and licks Georges's hand. Georges does not move.

INT. GEORGES'S ROOM. NIGHT

Georges puts a record on an old-fashioned turntable. On the sleeve, a smiling reproduction of Luis Mariano's face. The song starts up. Georges lies on his bed and mouths the words. Luis Mariano's voice fits his lips.

LUIS MARIANO'S VOICE
Maman, c'est toi la plus belle du monde,
Aucune autre à la ronde n'est plus jolie
Tu as pour moi, avoue que c'est étrange
Le visage d'un ange du paradis . . .[1]

The face of a white-haired woman approaches Georges's face. She kisses his forehead. Georges is delighted. He opens his eyes. The old lady, who is Georges's Mum, sits on the edge of his bed. Georges hugs her tight. She takes him in her arms.

GEORGES
Mum.

MUM
How is my big boy?

GEORGES
I don't want to stay here, Mum . . . I want to go home.

MUM
You know that's not possible, my darling.

He takes her hand and puts it on his cheek. He lays his head on her breast.

1 Mum, you are the loveliest in the world,
No one else around looks better than you
To me, your face, strange to say,
Is the face of an angel in paradise . . .

My baby . . . my tiny little baby . . .

GEORGES

Me sleep in your bed?

MUM

You've got your own bed now. It's time you were a big boy . . .

GEORGES

I don't want to . . . I want to go in your bed . . .

Georges's Mum gives him a hug and strokes his cheek.

I want to go home, I do.

MUM

Maybe one day you'll leave and . . .

GEORGES

. . . then I'll find a woman and marry.

MUM

Perhaps . . .

GEORGES

Me like everyone else. I'll watch and do the same as everyone.

MUM

Good Georges . . . I'm proud of you.

Georges's Mum's hand strokes Georges's cheek and pauses. He examines the hand. We move away . . . He is sitting alone in bed, examining his own hand. His mother has vanished.

EXT. INSTITUTE GROUNDS. DAY

Georges is sitting on a bench with his case, staring at the gates. After a bit, he stands and picks up his case. He crosses the lawns and walks towards the gates. A dog catches up with him. They walk out of the gates. Beyond: open countryside.

EXT. ROAD. DAY

A crossroads. Georges examines a large arrow painted on the ground. He stares in the direction of the arrow. He starts to walk. We rise above enormous arrow on the tarmac . . . Georges and his dog march along the deserted road.

INT. HARRY'S SITTING-ROOM. NIGHT

Harry strolls through his empty room, carrying a glass. The remains of a pizza lie on the table. He mumbles to himself, slightly the worse for wear.

> HARRY
> I've done nothing wrong . . . I'm . . . I'm not to blame. It wasn't my fault. I'm not saying it's yours. No . . .

As he says this, he turns to face an empty armchair: he is talking to an empty armchair.

> I'm only doing what people seem to expect of me. Grinning and bearing it. At first, we were happy, we were broke, we had pasta for supper every day. Now all I can do is grab some frozen pizza at two in the morning.

He looks towards the empty armchair. Then he turns his back on it.

> You shouldn't have left like that without a word. I didn't want you to go without saying why.

> JULIE
> I don't know why I did.

Harry turns round. Julie is right there, sitting in the armchair. She has her coat across her knees and a travel bag by her side.

> HARRY
> Julie!

> JULIE
> I swear I'd say if I knew what went wrong. But . . . I don't know . . . It's not your fault. It's me. It's me . . . I'm scared my life could turn out to be no different from what it has been . . .

> HARRY
> What do you mean, what it has been?

> JULIE
> (*indicating the room*)
> This . . . I need . . . to find out who I am . . . Me . . .

26

HARRY

But you are . . . but you are you . . . you . . .

JULIE

No . . .

HARRY

You have to believe in yourself, you . . .

JULIE

Don't try your method with me, Harry. It only works for
selling things. You've turned into your method. You've been
playing that game for so long now, it's swallowed you up . . .

HARRY

Julie . . .

He comes towards her on his knees.

JULIE

Don't touch me, Harry.

HARRY

Julie . . .

He holds out his hand.

JULIE

Please don't touch me. Your hands burn.

*Suddenly she is gone. Harry is on his own, on his knees, beside an
empty armchair.*

INT. HARRY'S BEDROOM. DAY

The alarm clock moves to 7.30.

RADIO PRESENTER'S VOICE

Today's Monday. It's 7.30. The temperature is 16 degrees
centigrade. An area of low pressure . . .

EXT. HARRY'S STREET. DAY

The garage door opens automatically. The car emerges.

INT. MEETING-ROOM. DAY

Harry is all undone. He stands in a corner away from the group, trying to get a coffee machine to work. His temper snaps. He shakes the machine, gives it a thump. A piece of the machine breaks off. Harry's colleagues turn and stare. Embarrassed, Harry leaves.

INT. HARRY'S OFFICE

Harry gathers up the papers on his desk and picks up his jacket. He passes Bruno.

> HARRY
> I can't get anything done. I'm going to take a couple of days at home to write that speech.

He leaves.

EXT. TOYSHOP. DAY

A teddy bear in the window of a toyshop. Harry enters the shop.

EXT. MOTORWAY. DAY

Harry drives down the motorway. The teddy bear lies on the back seat.

EXT. JULIE'S STREET. EVENING

Beside the sea-dyke. Harry's car is parked at a corner. He is behind the wheel, watching his two children, Alice and Juliette, play on the dyke. They do not notice him.

The girls go inside.

Harry does not move. He shuts his eyes.

EXT. COUNTRY ROAD. NIGHT

The teddy bear lies on the back seat. Harry drives down a dead-straight country road. It's raining.

Harry looks up the straight road. His eyes close. Slowly, he lets go of the wheel. The car carries on. His eyes are closed, his hands an inch or two from the wheel. The road runs by.

A thud. A black shape rolls against the windscreen. Harry jerks the wheel and slams on the brakes. The car spins round. The world goes still. Silence.

Harry tries to pull himself together. He checks the rear-view mirror. He gets out of the car. A few yards away, on the empty road, a black dog lying on its side, motionless. Nothing but fields around.

Harry approaches the dog. A synthesized voice comes from the car.

SYNTHESIZED VOICE

Your door is open – your door is open . . .

Harry approaches the dog. He touches it gingerly, then wipes his fingers on his handkerchief. He turns round and steps back suddenly, unable to stifle a cry. A man stares at him. This is Georges. Harry swallows hard. Georges stares at him even more. Rain runs down his face. He does not brush it away. Harry calms himself down.

HARRY

Is the dog yours? I . . . I didn't see it coming . . . I'm very sorry . . .

Georges does not move.

Do you . . . understand? The dog . . . Didn't see . . . Braked too late.

Georges goes to the dog, kneels down, strokes its head.

I'll take you home.

Harry opens the boot of his car, takes out a blanket and wraps the dog in it. Then he lifts the dog into the car. He holds the passenger door open for Georges. Georges gets in the car, with his suitcase on his knee. He looks around. Harry gets in beside him.

Where do you live?

No reply.

Do you speak French?
                              (*In English*)
Do you speak English?

This sentence obtains a response.

GEORGES
(*in English*)

My table is yellow . . .

HARRY
(*in French*)

Pardon?
                              (*In English*)
My name is Harry. What is your name?

GEORGES
(*in English*)

My name is John.

HARRY
(*in English*)

Where do you live, John?

GEORGES
(*in English*)

John and Mary are married. They have two children.

Harry can't tell what to make of this. He starts shouting.

HARRY
(*in English*)
WHERE DO YOU LIVE?

Georges frowns and shouts back.

GEORGES
(*in French*)
I'M NOT DEAF!

Pause.

HARRY
(*in French*)
You speak French? Where do you live?

GEORGES
Rue des Cerisiers, number 18.

HARRY
Is that nearby?

GEORGES
I'm hungry, I am.

Harry is puzzled. He starts the car.

EXT. POLICE STATION. NIGHT

A deserted street in the suburbs. Harry stops the car by the blue light of a police station. He gets out and opens the door for Georges.

HARRY
Come on. They'll know what to do here.

Georges remains in the car. He is knitting.

INT. POLICE STATION. NIGHT

Harry enters the police station. There is only one Policeman. He is typing behind the counter.

HARRY
I've found someone. I've brought him here. He's a bit . . . handicapped, I think.

POLICEMAN

Bring him in.

HARRY

He won't leave the car. He says he's hungry.

POLICEMAN

I can't leave, I'm on duty. If the phone rings and I'm not here
. . . see? I've got a ham sandwich if he wants it. Bring him in.

EXT. POLICE STATION. NIGHT

Harry tries to get Georges out. Georges won't budge. He's busy knitting.

HARRY

Get out! I can't deal with you . . . They've got a ham
sandwich in there you can have.

INT. POLICE STATION. NIGHT

Harry is at the counter. He is losing his temper . . .

HARRY

He's just outside.

POLICEMAN

I can't leave the station. You can see I'm on my own. Come
back tomorrow morning.

HARRY

And what am I supposed to do with him between now and
tomorrow morning? He lives in the rue des Cerisiers.

POLICEMAN

There's a rue des Cerisiers about a mile from here.

He returns to his typing. Harry cannot believe this is happening.

HARRY

It's not my problem. You've got to look after him. YOU
HAVE GOT TO LOOK AFTER HIM. THAT'S WHAT
WE PAY TAXES FOR!

Furious, the Policeman stands and follows Harry out.

EXT. POLICE STATION. NIGHT

Harry leaves the police station, followed by the Policeman. He goes to the car. Georges is no longer in the passenger seat. Harry's gaze searches for him. The street is deserted.

POLICEMAN

Well? Where is he?

HARRY

Well . . . Gone.

The Policeman goes back inside. Harry is puzzled. He stares down the empty street. He gets back in the car and drives off.

EXT. SUBURBAN STREET. NIGHT

Harry at the wheel, driving. Georges's head appears behind him, from the back seat. Georges remains silent. The teddy bear is on his knees. Harry has not noticed.

GEORGES

I don't like ham.

Harry jumps and slams on the brakes. The car stops. He turns to Georges.

HARRY

What are you doing there, John? Leave that alone! It belongs to my daughter.

GEORGES

Me not John! Me Georges! Rue des Cerisiers, number 18.

Harry reclaims the bear. Georges is knitting.

EXT. WASTELAND. NIGHT

A sign marked 'Rue des Cerisiers' stuck in an empty street surrounded by wasteland. There are no houses. Harry's car stops. He gets out and looks around, puzzled. Georges does not move.

HARRY

Are you sure you live in the rue des Cerisiers?

GEORGES

Number 18, rue des Cerisiers. It is not here.

Georges opens his suitcase full of treasures. He extracts an oil painting. It shows a pretty house marked number 18, in front of which stands a lady (Georges's mother) and a teenage girl. Georges shows Harry the picture.

GEORGES

Georges's house. Georges's mum. Georges's sister.

Harry examines the picture. He's puzzled.

HARRY

Rue des Cerisiers in Brussels?

GEORGES

What?

HARRY

In Brussels?

Georges seems less sure of himself.

GEORGES

That I don't know.

Harry sighs. He rests against the car, discouraged.

GEORGES

I live at rue des Cerisiers, number 18.

HARRY

In what town?

Harry opens Georges's door.

Get out of the car.

Georges shuts the door. Harry opens the boot and looks at the dog wrapped in a blanket. He sighs and slams the boot closed.

EXT. HARRY'S GARDEN. NIGHT

Harry, in shirtsleeves, digging a deep hole at the bottom of his garden. The house is all lit up. Harry takes the dog wrapped in a blanket and slides it into the hole. Georges watches him. Harry picks up a shovel and refills the hole.

Georges does not move. He holds his hands together over his chest in prayer. His voice suddenly breaks out into a strident religious hymn.

> GEORGES
> GO-OO-OO-OO-OO-OOOD AAAALLLLLMI-I-I-IGHTY
> GO-OO-OO-OO-OO-OOOD AAAALLLLLMI-I-I-IGHTY,
> SUCH A LOVER-ER-ER-LY WED-D-D-D-DING,
> OH GO-OD.

Georges's voice in the night. Dogs bark in the distance. Harry looks at him, covers him in a blanket.

A man in a dressing-gown looks over the hedge from the neighbouring garden. Harry is a little embarrassed.

> HARRY
> Good evening, doctor.

> DOCTOR
> Good evening. Is everything all right?

> HARRY
> Yes, thank you, doctor.

Harry smiles foolishly. The neighbour disappears.

INT. HARRY'S SITTING-ROOM. NIGHT

Harry puts a blanket and a pillow on his couch. Outside, the singing comes to a halt. He goes to the window.

EXT. HARRY'S GARDEN/HARRY'S NEIGHBOUR'S GARDEN. NIGHT

Georges is no longer at the bottom of the garden. Harry goes down. He finds the blanket on the grass. Over the hedge, he catches sight of Georges in the next-door garden, beside a swimming-pool. Gently, Georges puts a foot on the water.

> HARRY
> Hey! N. –

Harry freezes. He stares . . . Georges has put his second foot on the

water . . . He does not sink . . . He is walking on the water . . .
Several steps . . .

Harry cannot believe this. He watches, open-mouthed . . . Georges
crosses over to the side and returns towards Harry's house.

Harry goes over the hedge somewhat nervously. He makes his way to the
pool, bends down and reaches out . . . He finds an insulating sheet an inch
or two below the surface of the water. Harry sighs and lets go of the sheet.

INT. HARRY'S SITTING-ROOM. NIGHT

Harry returns to his house . . . Wet footsteps lead across the sitting-
room. Harry follows them.

INT. HARRY'S BATHROOM. NIGHT

Georges, wearing pyjamas, is brushing his teeth, wearing a towelling
dressing-gown.

> HARRY
> Hey! That's *my* toothbrush.

He grabs his toothbrush and waves it in Georges's face.

> My toothbrush! My bathroom! My dressing-gown! My
> pyjamas! My house! Harry's.

> GEORGES
> Yes. Me too toothbrush! Georges's house.

He turns on the tap at the washbasin and sprays water everywhere. He
combs his hair back and looks at himself admiringly in the mirror.
Showbiz smile.

> Nice hair to visit Mum.

He leaves. Harry wipes the floor with a sponge.

INT. HARRY'S SITTING-ROOM. NIGHT

Harry crosses the sitting-room. He is looking for Georges but can't find
him.

INT. CHILDREN'S ROOM. NIGHT

Harry goes into the children's room. It is dark. Georges is lying in Alice's bed, surrounded by soft toys and Mickey Mouse dolls, with his eyes closed. Harry looks at Georges with something approaching tenderness. He sits on the edge of the bed. Georges takes hold of Harry's hand. Harry shrinks back, then decides to go with it. Georges falls asleep. His breathing grows regular. Harry stands up quietly.

INT. HARRY'S BEDROOM. DAWN

Daybreak. Harry opens his eyes. A loud voice from the living-room.

> CHEF'S VOICE
> (*off-screen*)

Mix the custard, the cocoa, the sugar and a bit of milk. Bring the rest of the milk to the boil and pour it into the custard, stirring all the time . . .

INT. HARRY'S SITTING-ROOM. DAY

The TV is bellowing into an empty room. Harry switches it off. He steps on the contents of a pot of jam on the floor.

INT. HARRY'S KITCHEN. DAY

The kitchen is topsy-turvy. The fridge is wide open. A bottle of milk is spilled on the floor. Harry sees the table is covered in chocolate wrappers. Two whole bars of chocolate have been devoured.

INT. CHILDREN'S ROOM. DAY

Harry pushes the door of the children's room. Georges is asleep on the floor. He seems to be having trouble breathing. Harry lifts him up. Georges does not open his eyes. His breathing is irregular and rough.

INT. HARRY'S SITTING-ROOM. DAY

Harry's neighbour – the doctor – still wearing his dressing-gown, fills a syringe. Georges lies inanimate on the couch. The doctor gives him an injection.

DOCTOR

What's he been eating?

HARRY

Two whole chocolate bars, a pot of jam, two rolls.

DOCTOR

He's in shock, anaphylactic shock, as a result of some allergy, probably chocolate.

The doctor gives him a look. Georges opens his eyes.

DOCTOR

Are you on a diet?

Georges rubs his eyes.

GEORGES

No chocolate, Georges! Not good.

DOCTOR

Chocolate? (*He waves his finger at him, as at a child.*) No chocolate, ever. Never! (*To Harry*) Your friend needs watching.

HARRY

He isn't my friend.

The doctor is somewhat intrigued. He shuts his case. Harry walks him to the door and takes out his wallet.

DOCTOR

There's no charge. But do try to stop him eating chocolate.

The doctor leaves. Harry turns round. Georges is no longer in the room. The telephone rings. The answering-machine goes on.

ANSWERING-MACHINE

This is Bruno . . . I know you are working at home today, but the Director wants you to accompany our client when he visits the location of the annual general meeting . . .

Harry sighs.

INT. CHILDREN'S ROOM. DAY

Harry goes into the children's room. He sees the cupboard door shut. He tries to open it, but it won't budge.

HARRY
What are you doing in there! Come on out!

GEORGES
No. Me go to Mum's. Rue des Cerisiers, number 18.

Harry leaves and returns with the phone book. He turns the pages.

HARRY
You're going to tell me whether any of these names mean anything to you, OK? Alost, Andenne, Antwerp, Arlon, Ath, Baasrode, Bastogne . . .

He glances at the door. It has still not budged.

Bastogne? . . . Beauraing, Beauvechain, Bellevaux, Bergen, Bertrix, Binche . . . Bois Robert, Braibant, Bruges, Brussels, Carlsbourg, Cerfontaine, Chapelle . . .

The cupboard opens.

Chapelle?

Georges's smiling face appears.

It's not exactly round the corner.

INT. HARRY'S KITCHEN. DAY

A slice of toast jumps out of the toaster.

INT. HARRY'S BATHROOM. DAY

The toothbrush drops back into the glass. Georges smiles at his reflection.

EXT. HARRY'S STREET. DAY

The automatic door to the garage opens and Harry's car emerges. Georges is next to Harry.

EXT. CITY STREET WITH SHOPS. DAY

Georges is in the car. On his knees, the painting of his mother's house. The car stops at a red light. The light is red for pedestrians too. Georges stares at one of them. He shakes his hand through the window.

> GEORGES

Hello. My name's Georges.

The Pedestrian is disconcerted.

Me go to Mum's. Rue des Cerisiers, number 18.

> PEDESTRIAN

Really?

> GEORGES

I love the tie. (*He points to the pedestrian's tie.*) Me buy nice clothes too, surprise for Mum. Nice suit, nice shoes.

Georges notices a shoeshop.

Lovely shoes!

He gets out of the car and leaves the door open.

> HARRY

Hey!

The lights change to green. Cars honk. Harry closes the door and finds somewhere to park. Georges has vanished.

INT. SHOESHOP. DAY

Georges enters the shop. He examines the shoes on display. A Saleswoman arrives.

> SALESWOMAN

Can I help you?

She smiles, then looks astonished. Georges looks her up and down with delight.

> GEORGES

Me want shoes.

Georges makes for the shelves. He takes a pair of high-heeled shoes.

SALESWOMAN

For you, sir?

Georges nods. He is examining some sports shoes.

GEORGES

Ah. Tennis shoes.

SALESWOMAN

Take a seat. I'll fetch them for you.

She leaves. Georges sits down. Harry appears and stares at Georges through the display window. He signals that Georges should leave. The Saleswoman returns. She removes Georges's shoes and puts the tennis shoes on him. She pulls his socks up. Georges smiles with pleasure at the touch of her hand on his skin.

They are very pretty.

GEORGES

You are very pretty too, Miss.

He looks her in the eye. She moves back. He takes her by the hand.

Me like to do marriage with you.

The Saleswoman removes her hand.

SALESWOMAN

Will you keep them on or shall I wrap them up?

GEORGES

Do marriage with you.

SALESWOMAN

I'm married already.

GEORGES

Doesn't matter, me too. You two eyes, two ears, two hands, two lovers.

The Saleswoman has got to her feet. She is entering the price on the till.

Seven hundred francs.

Georges empties his pockets on the counter. He leaves some paper, shells and a few coins there. The Saleswoman counts the coins.

Twenty-six francs. You've only got twenty-six francs.

Georges leans on the counter. It is clear he is not leaving.

GEORGES
Me want shoes.

SALESWOMAN
I can't give them to you if you've no money.

Georges sighs. He raises his voice.

GEORGES
ME WANT SHOES!

The Saleswoman goes off into the back room. Harry enters the shop. He pulls at Georges's arm.

Me want shoes.

The Manager arrives, followed by the Saleswoman. He gives a great big commercial smile.

MANAGER
(*to Harry*)
What kind of shoes are you looking for?

HARRY
He's the one who wants the shoes.

The Manager looks at Georges.

MANAGER
(*to Harry*)
Ah. And what kind of shoes is he looking for?

HARRY
Ask him.

The Manager is bemused. Georges rummages through the shop. He touches everything. A woman customer enters. The Manager comes up to Harry. He speaks softly, without losing his smile.

> MANAGER

Get out of my shop.

> HARRY

Excuse me?

> MANAGER
> (*lower, threatening*)

Get him out of my shop.

> HARRY

Your smile is insincere. A good salesman's smile is always sincere. And if there's one thing I can't stand, it's a bad salesman.

Georges comes back to the counter and leans on it.

> GEORGES

Me want shoes.

The Saleswoman can't take any more. She stuffs the shoes into a bag.

> SALESWOMAN

Here. Take them.

Georges smiles radiantly. He pulls her towards him, looks as if he is about to give her a kiss on the cheek, but at the last moment he pecks her on the neck.

> GEORGES

Thank you very much!

Proudly, he leaves the store. Harry takes out his wallet and puts two banknotes on the counter before leaving.

EXT. CITY STREET WITH SHOPS. DAY

Georges is waiting by the car. As Harry appears, Georges proudly displays the bag.

GEORGES
(*in English*)

In the pocket.

HARRY

If you're going to buy something, you have to pay for it first.
Do you understand me? And if you've no money, then you
mustn't start buying things.

GEORGES

I have money.

*Georges gets into the car, opens his case and pulls out a piggy bank,
which he shakes to show it is full.*

HARRY

Well, why didn't you pay for the shoes, then?

GEORGES

But this is Georges's!

He shuts the piggy bank safely away in his case. Harry starts the car.

EXT. STREET OUTSIDE AN OFFICE BLOCK. DAY

*The car stops in a car park at the foot of the building in which Harry
has his office. Harry gets out of the car.*

HARRY

I'll be two minutes. You wait here.

INT. LECTURE THEATRE. DAY

*Harry enters a large auditorium. Workmen are putting up a huge
'Delta Bank' sign above the stage. The Director and the clients are
leaving the room. Harry follows them.*

EXT. OFFICE BLOCK ROOF. DAY

*They reach the roof. Technicians bring up crates. Others lay electrical
cables. In the background, the Director is explaining.*

DIRECTOR

The colours of the fireworks match the new logo . . .

Harry leans over the safety rail. At the foot of the building, he sees Georges leave the car and cross the street. Harry rushes to the stairs.

EXT. OFFICE BLOCK/CHOCOLATE SHOP/CAR. DAY

Harry runs. He sees Georges across the street outside a chocolate shop. Open-mouthed, Georges is staring at the display, which is full of magnificent heart-shaped boxes.

                    HARRY
No chocolate. Come on. We're leaving . . .

                    GEORGES
No. Want chocolate.

Georges is in ecstasy. He bites his lip. He thumps his head against the window. Harry goes inside. Georges sees Harry buy an enormous box. Then Harry exits, unwraps the box under Georges's nose. Georges stares at the pralines, completely entranced. Harry backs towards the car holding the box out to Georges. Georges follows him, hypnotized.

                    HARRY
Come on . . .

Harry slides in behind the wheel, still holding the chocolates out to Georges. Georges gets in the car. Harry starts the engine and the car tears off. Georges reaches out for the chocolates. Harry chucks the box out of the window. Georges lets out a cry and watches the box fall into the road. The chocolates scatter.

                    GEORGES
HEEEEEEEEEY!

He stares furiously at Harry.

                    HARRY
No chocolate, Georges! You know that!

Georges grabs the telephone off the dashboard, yanks out the wire and throws the lot out of the window. The telephone is run over by a car. Harry cannot believe this is happening.

                    GEORGES
Harry is mean.

That's right.

Silence. They are both in a sulk.

GEORGES
(*between gritted teeth*)

Cunt.

HARRY

What? What was that?

GEORGES

Cunt. Faggot. Bugger. Homo. Arsehole. Bastard.

Harry stares at him in surprise.

Mongol!

HARRY

Hey! You're the mongol.

GEORGES

Mongol.

HARRY

Mongol.

Georges smiles.

GEORGES

Yes, me mongol. Tee-hee.

Georges gives Harry a great friendly slap on the back. He puts his head on Harry's shoulder. Harry relaxes.

My mate Harry.

EXT. ROAD. DAY

The car drives down the road. Music. White dotted line runs beside the car. Georges is happy. He holds the picture of his mother's house on his knees. He looks out of the window with a smile. He puts his head back. The trees pass by above him, making near-abstract patterns against a blue sky. Georges opens the window. Wind blows through his hair. He stretches out his arm to feel the wind in his fingers.

Georges pretends he is the driver. He copies every one of Harry's gestures. Harry overtakes a butcher's truck. Georges puts out an arm and gives the driver the finger.

                    HARRY
Hey!

Behind, the truck driver honks and flashes his lights. He speeds up threateningly. Harry speeds up too. Georges gives the truck the finger again. Harry yanks Georges inside. They end up pulling away.

I've got enough problems as it is.

                    GEORGES
What problems?

                    HARRY
My problems. *My* family. *My* work.

                    GEORGES
What? You work?

                    HARRY
Yes.

                    GEORGES
Why?

                    HARRY
To earn my living . . . to have some money . . . To pay for the car, to pay for my house.

                    GEORGES
Me don't work. Me handicapped. Me get money without working.

Georges smiles broadly. He pulls out his piggy bank and gives it to Harry.

For Harry.

                    HARRY
No.

                    GEORGES
Yes. Me want to help Harry.

47

Harry gives the piggy bank back. Georges rummages through his pockets, finds seashells, marbles, a few coins and slips the lot into Harry's pocket without Harry noticing. He looks at Harry, satisfied.

My mate Harry. Go on, give us a laugh.

Harry is in no mood to laugh. Georges forces a laugh.

Ha ha ha ha ha ha! Go on, give us a laugh! Ha ha ha ha ha!

Harry smiles. Georges laughs more.

Ha ha ha ha ha ha ha!

Harry starts to laugh too. The car crosses a broad landscape. Their laughter mixes in with the music.

EXT. RUE DES CERISIERS. DAY

The car drives through an area of small, oldish bungalows. The cherry trees are in blossom. Harry's car slows down beside a small house set in a patch of garden. Harry and Georges look at the painting. It's the same house all right. Georges gets out of the car and runs towards the house.

GEORGES
Mum! Mum!

Harry follows him, holding the picture. Georges rings the bell.

The door opens. An Indian Man wearing a turban appears. He and Georges exchange an astonished glance.

INDIAN MAN
Yes?

Georges's expression hardens. He spins round and returns to the car. Harry watches him, then looks at the Indian Man.

HARRY
Excuse me. Did an elderly lady live here? This lady . . .

He shows the picture. The Indian Man puts on his spectacles and examines the painting.

INDIAN MAN

Ah yes. Yes indeed . . . But . . . the lady died. Four years ago. We bought the house.

Harry is surprised. Georges is sitting motionless in the car. He is waiting for them to drive off.

I've got a forwarding address for the daughter.

He vanishes into the house and returns with a scrap of paper on which an address is scrawled.

Georges is waiting in the car. Harry joins him. Georges seems sad.

GEORGES

Mummy dead. Mummy heaven.

HARRY
(*furious*)

Four years ago. You knew. Didn't you?

GEORGES

I forgot.

Harry checks the scrap of paper.

EXT. COUNTRY ROAD. DAY

Harry is driving. He's tired. Georges is fiddling with the radio, pressing buttons. Classical music . . . He switches . . . A chat show. Some comedians are telling jokes.

RADIO COMEDIAN

. . . so then the other one says, 'My bike is at home, I left it there.'

Laughter. Applause. Georges laughs along.

GEORGES

Ha ha ha! My bike is at home! Ha ha ha!

He glances at Harry, who is not laughing. Georges switches the radio off.

I know a joke. Two madmen paint a ceiling. One takes away the ladder. 'Hey, hold on to the ladder, I'm taking the brush away.'

HARRY

Hold on to the brush, I'm taking the ladder.

GEORGES

What?

HARRY

He says, 'Hold on to the brush . . .'

GEORGES

No, ladder. He says 'ladder'.

HARRY

He says 'brush', otherwise it wouldn't be funny.

Georges loses his temper.

GEORGES

HE SAYS 'HOLD ON TO THE LADDER'. IT'S VERY FUNNY. A JOKE.

Silence. They are both in a sulk. Georges is sad. They slow down. A truck is in front, driving very slowly. The same butcher's truck as before, the one Georges gave the finger to.

Georges presses down on the horn.

HARRY

Hey!

Harry overtakes the truck. Georges lowers his window and gives the driver the finger again. The driver honks angrily. He speeds up and comes up right against the back bumper of Harry's car, flashing his lights. Suddenly, the truck overtakes them and stops dead. Harry pulls over and slams on the brakes. The truck blocks the road. Harry has gone pale.

GEORGES

He's crazy!

Georges sounds the horn again. Harry furiously pushes him away. The truck driver comes out of his truck and walks towards the car.

HARRY
(*to Georges*)

Whatever you do, don't say anything!

Harry comes out of the car. He looks very apologetic.

I'm sorry, he didn't mean . . .

The driver grabs Harry. Georges is panic-struck. He locks his door. The automatic locking system then locks all four doors. Harry runs to the car and tries to get his door open. It's locked. He shakes it. Georges looks elsewhere, so as not to see what is going on. The driver flips Harry round and puts a fist in his face. Harry's face squashes against the glass. His nose is bleeding. Georges looks away, with a mild expression of pain. He closes his eyes. He doesn't know what to do . . . he turns the radio on. Cheerful music bellows out: a game show.

RADIO PRESENTER'S VOICE

And it's five points! Congratulations! (*Applause*) Now do you want to use your joker for the *twenty-point* question? Do you! Here's the question: who sang the song 'Who knows? Who knows?' in 1949? You're into the countdown . . .

GEORGES

Luis Mariano.

The driver lifts Harry up. No outside sound is audible inside the car. Only the game-show clock counting down. Georges yells at the radio.

IT'S LUIS MARIANO!

RADIO PRESENTER'S VOICE

'Ding dong!' The right answer was Luis Mariano!

'Qui sait, qui sait', one of Luis Mariano's songs, echoes around the car. Georges mouths the words. He hides his eyes, so as not to see what is going on. Then he takes up his needles and yarn and starts knitting. The truck takes off. Harry picks himself up. He takes a handkerchief out of his pocket and dabs at his nose. He comes back towards the car. Georges looks sheepish. Harry is furious. He knocks at the window, signalling to Georges that he should pull the locking device up. Georges does as he is told.

GEORGES

I won, I did. It was Luis Mariano.

Harry glares at Georges and snaps the radio off.

Hey!

                          HARRY
Don't say anything! Whatever you do, just don't say anything.

He drives off.

EXT. COUNTRY ROAD. DAY

The car slows on a straight country road. Dark clouds in the sky. A bus stop. Harry stops the car. He gets out and opens Georges's door. Georges does not budge.

                          HARRY
Come on. Out.

Georges does not get out.

This is it. You're getting out here.

He yanks Georges. Shamefacedly, Georges extricates himself from the car. Harry takes the case and puts it down at Georges's feet. He puts the piece of paper with Georges's sister's address on it in Georges's hand and holds the hand up in the air.

Go there. Understand? It's your sister's address.

He shoves a few bank notes in Georges's pocket.

And find yourself another sucker.

Georges remains immobile, open-mouthed, his hand in the air. Harry slams the car door and starts the engine. Georges remains alone on the side of the road, beside his suitcase. The car drives off.

EXT. COUNTRY ROAD. DAY

Harry drives as fast as he can. He undoes his tie-knot.

EXT. COUNTRY ROAD. DAY

Georges has not moved. Thunder sounds in the distance. He looks up at the sky. A drop of rain splashes down on to his forehead and runs down his face.

EXT. COUNTRY ROAD. DAY

A few raindrops squash against the windscreen. Harry takes a cigarette and puts it to his lips. He rummages through his pockets looking for a light. His wallet drops out and a picture of his children falls from it. Harry is touched by the picture. He puts it back in his wallet. His hand feels deeper into his pocket. He finds the seashells Georges gave him.

EXT. COUNTRY ROAD. DAY

In the distance, a bus. Georges stares at it, his hand still in the air. The bus slows down and stops. The door opens right by Georges. Georges stares right ahead. The bus waits. Georges does not move. The bus door closes.

EXT. COUNTRY ROAD, DAY

Harry glances at the shells in the palm of his hand. His car is stopped beside the road. Rain hammers down dully on the windscreen. Harry can't decide what to do. He stares at the shells. And turns the car round.

EXT. COUNTRY ROAD. DAY

It is raining hard. Harry drives slowly. The road is hardly visible for rain. Harry slows down. He sees Georges standing like a statue, hand in the air, exactly where he left him. Georges has not budged.

> **HARRY**
> Georges!

Georges is soaked through. His face lights up at the sight of Harry. Harry runs towards him and throws his mac across his shoulders.

> **GEORGES**
> Harry! I knew you'd be back.

> **HARRY**
> Put this on! Can't you see it's raining?

Georges looks Harry in the eye, taking no notice of the rain on his face. He is radiantly happy.

> **GEORGES**
> So you do like me!

53

Georges's face lights up. Harry does not know what to say. Georges puts his arms around Harry and hugs him. At first Harry keeps his hands in the air, not knowing what to do.

My mate Harry! I knew it!

Harry's hands descend slowly to land on Georges's shoulders. Harry hugs Georges. Georges is laughing he is so happy. He puts his forehead on Harry's forehead. Rain pours down their faces.

My mate Harry! Ha ha!

Harry takes a handkerchief and wipes away the rain from Georges's face.

EXT. COUNTRY ROAD. DAY

Georges's eyes are closed. He smiles peacefully. His head rests on Harry's shoulder as Harry drives. The scrap of paper lies crumpled on the dashboard. Georges's eyes open. The rain gives way to sunshine. Georges sees Luis Mariano sitting on the bonnet, wearing his sequin costume.

LUIS MARIANO
(*singing*)
L'amour est un bouquet de violettes,
L'amour est plus doux que ces fleurettes,
Quand le bonheur en passant vous fait signe et s'arrête
Il faut lui prendre la main sans attendre à demain.[1]

Luis Mariano's hair blows in the wind. He smiles at Georges. Georges closes his eyes. Luis Mariano's voice rocks him. His Mum's face caresses his face. He turns round. She is in the back seat, smiling. Georges smiles at the road and moves to the sound of the music.

EXT. CAR PARK. DAY

The car is beside a pay phone in an empty car park. Harry is making a call. Georges waits outside. In the booth, Harry dials.

1 Love is a bunch of violets,
Love is sweeter than blossom,
When happiness happens to beckon
Don't wait, take it by the hand.

INT. JULIE'S LIVING-ROOM. DAY

The phone rings. Sound of gulls outside. The children play. Julie's mother answers the phone.

EXT. CAR PARK. DAY

> JULIE'S MOTHER'S VOICE

Hello?

> HARRY

Julie?

> JULIE'S MOTHER'S VOICE

One moment. I'll get her.

> JULIE'S VOICE

Hello?

> HARRY

It's me.

> JULIE

Harry? I told you not to call.

Georges comes and stands before Harry. He stares at him. He presses his nose against the glass.

> HARRY

Is your mother staying with you?

> JULIE

I needed a hand.

> HARRY

I'd like . . . I just need to hear the sound of the children's voices.

> JULIE

They won't. You'll have to be patient.

Georges goes round to the other side of the booth and faces Harry again. He knocks on the window. Harry is absorbed. He signals to Georges that he should move away.

I'm in the neighbourhood. I could look in.

JULIE

Don't do that, Harry. We have an agreement. This is my place.

HARRY

What have I done to you?

JULIE

I don't want to talk about it. It is not your fault. It's me . . . I need . . . to get away from you.

Pause.

Goodbye.

HARRY

Wait! I've got a present for Alice, for her birthday.

JULIE

Your daughter's birthday is on the 14th.

HARRY

I can't come on the 14th. It's the day of the annual general meeting . . . There's nothing I can do about it. It's bad luck.

JULIE

No, it isn't.

Pause.

HARRY

That's why . . . I'm bringing the present early. I won't come in. Just let me . . .

JULIE

I won't open the door. Don't come. Don't call me.

She hangs up. Harry hangs up too. He comes out of the booth.

GEORGES

Who were you calling?

HARRY

My wife.

GEORGES

Oh. You're married. Where does she live?

HARRY

By the sea.

GEORGES

Is she pretty?

HARRY

I think so, yes.

GEORGES

You make love?

Harry does not reply. He hands Georges his knitting and starts the car.

EXT. GEORGES'S SISTER'S STREET. DAY

Identical, prefabricated bungalows. Georges folds his knitting into gift-wrap. Harry checks the address on the scrap of paper. He identifies a small, grey bungalow.

They get out of the car. Before they get to the door, it opens. A woman, Georges's sister, Fabienne, opens the door. She is surprised to see Georges.

FABIENNE

Georges?

Georges opens his arms wide and smiles.

GEORGES

Here I am.

Georges throws himself into his sister's arms and hugs her. She returns his embrace, but nervously. He tries to show her the present he has brought but she pays no attention.

FABIENNE

The institute called. What happened?

She sees Harry.

HARRY

Hello.

FABIENNE

What happened?

HARRY

I found him . . . He was lost, on a road . . . I've brought him
back . . .

Georges's sister seems embarrassed.

INT. SISTER'S LIVING-ROOM. DAY

*They enter the house. It is small and ordinary. The table is laid. A voice
comes from upstairs.*

FABIENNE'S HUSBAND

What is it, Fabienne?

*Fabienne's husband comes downstairs. He sees Georges and stops in his
tracks. Georges's smile fades. The husband's expression grows ominous.*

*Two children come downstairs: a boy and a girl aged five and eight.
They are delighted to see Georges.*

CHILDREN

Uncle Georges!

*They run circles around him, shouting and squealing. Georges playfully
tries to grab them.*

FABIENNE'S HUSBAND

QUIE-ET CHILDREN!

He catches them by the arm. They stop laughing.

FABIENNE

This gentleman found Georges on a road and brought him
here.

FABIENNE'S HUSBAND
(*to Harry*)
You're not going to leave him here?

FABIENNE

Alain . . .

FABIENNE'S HUSBAND
(*to his wife*)
He brought him. He can take him away again.

The sister sits Georges down and sits down beside him. She puts her arm around him and looks serious. She speaks kindly.

FABIENNE
Listen, Georges. You know you can't stay here. It always goes wrong. And then we both get upset. The best would be for your friend to take you back to the institute.

GEORGES

No! *My* sister!

He shoves the husband away and puts his head on Fabienne's thigh. She tries to get his head up. But he doesn't want that. He clings on to the tablecloth.

FABIENNE

Georges . . .

Georges tugs. His sister grabs the other end of the tablecloth to stop the crockery from falling.

GEORGES!!

Georges yells and pulls as hard as he can. His sister lets go. The crockery smashes on the floor. Harry catches as much as he can mid-air. Fabienne's husband grabs Georges from behind and holds him by the waist. Georges puts up a fight. They roll on to the floor. Harry tries to stops the husband. The children run around shrieking.

CHILDREN

Mum! Mum!

Georges is unable to move. His sister looks him in the eye.

FABIENNE
I'm fond of you, Georges, but I've given you all I could. I've got a new life now. I have my children, I have Alain. You've got to understand that.

GEORGES
Not nice. Mum said you be nice to Georges. I'll tell Mum.
Me don't want institute. Me stay here.

FABIENNE
Mum always looked after you. Who looked after me?

Georges looks at her in surprise. Fabienne is about to burst into tears.

I want a *life*. This is *my* life. *I cannot* look after *you*. I told
Mum. I told Mum I would not look after you. I told her.

Fabienne bursts into tears, her face in her hands. Georges looks sheepish.
No one moves. The children are astonished.

FABIENNE'S HUSBAND
Go to your room, children.

The children reluctantly go upstairs. Georges goes to Fabienne. He takes
his sister in his arms affectionately.

GEORGES
But I love you! I love you, little sister!

He gives her a big, consoling hug. She lets herself go.

Dear little Fabienne . . .

Fabienne's husband watches with Harry. Neither of them knows what to do. They exchange a look. The husband is on the verge of tears. He leaves the room, pulling a handkerchief out of his pocket. Sound of him blowing his nose in the kitchen.

EXT. SISTER'S STREET. DAY

Georges is in the car. He has taken his present back and holds it on his knee. Harry stands beside the car. Georges is in a sulk. His sister appears to say goodbye. She leans into the window. Georges stares straight ahead.

> FABIENNE
>
> Your friend has offered to take you back to the institute. OK? Goodbye, Georges.

> GEORGES
>
> Me not go institute. Me go on seaside holiday. With my mate Harry.

Fabienne gives Harry a card.

> FABIENNE
>
> This is the address.

Harry gets into the car. They drive off. Through the back window, the house disappears. Georges does not turn round.

> HARRY
>
> All right?

> GEORGES
>
> Say goodbye to the house.

> HARRY
>
> What?

> GEORGES
>
> Say goodbye to the house.

> HARRY
>
> Goodbye, house.

EXT. MOTORWAY BRIDGE. DAY

Georges stands on a bridge over the motorway watching the traffic stream past. Georges waves goodbye to the cars. The flow is uninterrupted. Georges looks sad. He turns to Harry.

> GEORGES
> Say goodbye to the cars . . .

> HARRY
> Goodbye, cars.

They stand side by side, waving goodbye to the cars. The cars fly past unaware. Harry sits on a building-site fence.

> GEORGES
> Me'd like to go to the seaside with Harry.

Harry holds up his index finger, slightly bent.

> HARRY
> Do you know what that is?

Georges glances vaguely in Harry's direction.

> It's a worm going round a bend.

Georges looks at Harry, straight-faced. Pause. Then the fence on which Harry is sitting collapses. Harry falls backwards. Georges bursts out laughing.

EXT. CAR PARK SNACK BAR. DAY

Harry parks the car in a car park just by a coffee shop. In the glove compartment he finds a pair of dark glasses. He puts them on Georges so that his slit eyes are no longer visible. He looks like one of the Blues Brothers. Harry straightens his tie-knot.

INT. COFFEE SHOP. DAY

Harry and Georges are seated on either side of a Formica table. Harry is cutting up George's meat. Georges is devouring a plateful of French fries. He stops the Waiter and shows him a fry. One tiny corner is burnt.

GEORGES

Burnt.

*The Waiter is astonished. He doesn't know what to do. Then he leaves.
Georges eats with his fingers. At another table, a little girl watches him
amazed. Georges smiles at her. The little girl drops her fork and starts
copying Georges, licking her fingers. Her father gives her a little slap on
the head. She goes back to her fork. The Waiter returns with a plate
upon which lies a single French fry, unburnt. A lovely Waitress brings
them their drinks. She seems very tired. On her way over, the Waiter
grumbles at her:*

WAITER

Table four hasn't been cleared.

WAITRESS

OK.

*She sighs and wipes the table clean. Georges examines her through his
dark glasses. He takes a flower in a vase and gives it to her. The
Waitress is touched. She smiles at him.*

Thank you. You're a kind person.

63

She returns to the kitchen. Georges remains still for a moment. Then he takes the knitting in its gift-wrap.

HARRY

Where are you going?

Georges goes to the kitchens. He pushes open the swing door.

INT. COFFEE-SHOP KITCHEN. DAY

Georges appears in the kitchen. Frying smoke, hamburgers hissing. He sees the Waitress and goes up to her. She is taken aback. He hands her his gift.

GEORGES

For you.

This surprises her even more, but she manages a smile.

WAITRESS

For me?

She gives him a look. He smiles at her. She smiles back. He removes his dark glasses. The waitress's expression changes. She steps back. She sees Georges's slit eyes. She hands him back the package.

I'm sorry . . . I didn't know . . . I . . . Excuse me.

She runs out through a back door.

INT. COFFEE SHOP. DAY

Georges returns to the dining-room. He stops, and is still. Harry gets up as soon as he sees him. Georges looks angry, put out. He rips open the package, tears at the knitting, throws it to the floor and stamps on it, yelling as he does. Harry tries to calm him down. Georges rolls around on the floor. He grabs at everything he can, screaming his despair. Harry lies on top of him to console him. He takes him in his arms. Georges hits at his own head with his fists, slaps himself, bites into his own hand . . . In the end, he quietens down and bursts into tears in Harry's arms.

HARRY

It's OK . . . it's OK . . .

Georges sobs desperately.

GEORGES

BUT I LOVE HER! I DO! . . . I LOVE HER! . . .

Harry holds him tight.

My mate . . . my mate . . .

EXT. ROAD. DAY

Georges's face against the window, staring into the distance. Tears run down his cheeks. His head shakes with every bump in the road. Georges glances down at the knitting in his lap. Slowly he tugs at the wool. It unravels. He winds it into a ball.

EXT. ROAD. EVENING

The car drives down a road along a river.

EXT. SEA. NIGHT

Night. Sound of the sea. Thick fog. Headlights light up the fog. Everything goes white. Harry's car stops. They get out. Harry stares into the whiteness.

> HARRY
>
> The sea is right there.

Georges stares around. Nothing but whiteness.

> GEORGES
>
> It's beautiful. Thank you, Harry.

Harry walks round the car. He looks down the road. Nothing is visible. He lights a cigarette.

Georges walks off into the fog. He can see no further than his feet. He goes into long grass.

By the car, Harry turns round. He has lost Georges. He takes a few steps. He's worried. He goes round to the other side of the car. He cups his hands to his mouth.

> HARRY
>
> Georges! . . .

Georges moves forwards through thick fog. He does not know where he is.

Sound of a horse's hoofs. Harry turns round. The sound fades into the distance.

Georges is walking away. He stops. In the fog, a horse stares at him without moving. A small Mongol horse in harness. The horse vanishes.

Georges walks on, watching his feet. He walks up the steps of a jetty. The sea is loud. He moves forwards. Suddenly, his mother's form appears in the fog beside him. She takes him by the arm.

> GEORGES
>
> Mum . . .

> MOTHER
>
> Watch out.

Georges looks down at his feet. The jetty comes to an end just where he is standing. He is on the brink of nothingness. He steps back. His mother is gone.

GEORGES

Mother?

Harry puts an arm into the car and starts honking.

Harry?

He runs towards the sound.

My friend Harry.

Harry hears Georges coming. He runs towards him. They collide and roll on to the frozen grass. They stare at each other. Georges laughs.

EXT. SEA-DYKE. DAY

Daybreak by the sea. The car is parked opposite the beach. A funfair, still under wraps, stands next to a caravan site. Harry and Georges are asleep in the car. Georges seems content. Close in on his face. Sound of a breeze and singing in the distance. The sun appears on his face.

EXT. MONGOLIA. DAY

A vast plain. A wind blows through high grass. A rider gallops up. We see his face: it's Georges. He is wearing a Mongol prince's costume.

EXT. SEA-DYKE. JULIE'S HOUSE. DAY

Georges wakes up. Harry turns towards a small house stuck between apartment blocks.

HARRY

Stay in the car . . .

GEORGES

Where are you going?

Harry approaches the house. He looks down at his shoes, his trousers. He looks unkempt. He rubs his face and smooths down his hair, coughs and rings the bell.

The door opens a crack. Julie's mother. She's about sixty. When she sees Harry, she closes the door. Harry rings insistently. He bangs on the door.

> JULIE'S MOTHER'S VOICE
>
> Please go.

He goes round the outside of the house. From the garden, he notices that one of the ground-floor windows is open. He climbs through it and goes inside.

INT. JULIE'S SITTING-ROOM. DAY

He comes through the sitting-room and calls out.

> HARRY
>
> JULIE! . . . ALICE! JULIETTE!

Julie's mother appears, waving her hands in the air.

> JULIE'S MOTHER
>
> Julie isn't here. Please, Harry. Go away before she comes back.

> HARRY
>
> JULIE!

The mother stands in his way. Suddenly, Julie is there, standing scared in the doorway. She is between thirty-five and forty, nice-looking but exhausted.

> JULIE'S MOTHER
>
> I couldn't stop him.

> HARRY
>
> Julie . . .

> JULIE
>
> Go away, Harry. This is my house.

> HARRY
>
> I've come to see my daughters. I've brought Alice her birthday present.

JULIE

The girls went to stay with a friend.

Julie opens the front door, signalling that Harry should leave. He goes towards the stairs instead. Julie stops him.

HARRY

ALICE! JULIETTE!

JULIE

Get out!

JULIE'S MOTHER

Just leave, Harry!

JULIE

Let me deal with this, Mum.

EXT. SEA-DYKE. JULIE'S HOUSE. DAY

Georges is bored in the car. He looks towards the house. He tries whistling through his fingers. Nothing happens. He honks.

Julie stands right in front of Harry.

> JULIE
>
> If you're not out of here within ten seconds, I don't know what I'll do. One . . . two . . . three . . .

Harry looks at Julie and starts to laugh.

> What are you laughing at?

> HARRY
>
> I don't know . . . Ha ha . . . It's so funny.

> JULIE
>
> I don't think it's funny.

He picks up a vase.

> Leave that.

> HARRY
>
> I bought this. Do you remember?

He drops it. It shatters on the ground. Julie starts to panic.

> JULIE
>
> Harry, get out! You're scaring me!

> HARRY
>
> Scaring you?

Harry gets down on all fours and moves towards Julie, making dog-like grunts. Julie does not know what to do. They chase round the table. Harry knocks chairs over as he goes. He grabs the tablecloth. Everything falls on the floor. Julie screams. Harry stands up and goes towards the stairs. Julie blocks his way.

> ALICE! ALICE!

> Let me by!

> JULIE
>
> Never!

He tries to get by anyway.

She shoves him back. He grabs her by the wrists. This hurts. She yanks an arm free. Harry moves towards Julie. He looks at her with tenderness.

HARRY

Oh, Julie . . .

He tries to take her in his arms. Julie struggles with him.

Julie . . . my darling . . .

JULIE

Leave me. Don't touch me.

She curls up into a ball. He tries to kiss her lovingly. She starts to cry.

DON'T TOUCH ME! Harry, please! Don't touch me. It burns.

She bursts into tears. Harry looks at her uncomprehendingly. He tries to get her to her feet. She takes hold of the poker and waves it at him. Harry steps back. She moves towards him menacingly.

HARRY

Oh, Julie. You shouldn't have done that.

She steps forwards again. He grabs her by the wrist and takes the poker. The mother starts yelling hysterically. Harry waves the poker. She shields her head. Harry looks at Julie and throws away the poker.

EXT. SEA-DYKE. JULIE'S HOUSE. DAY

Alice and Juliette appear on the pavement carrying a light bag. They see Harry's car.

ALICE

That's Daddy's car.

They go up to the car. Georges is waiting inside. Alice knocks on the window. Georges smiles and lowers the window.

Hello.

GEORGES

Hello.

71

Are you a friend of Dad's?

Georges just smiles.

Is he there?

GEORGES
Sssh! Surprise . . . Birthday.

He points to Alice.

ALICE
It isn't my birthday. My birthday's on the 14th.

GEORGES
Fourteenth?

ALICE
My daddy will come and fetch me on the 14th. Will you be there too?

GEORGES
OK.

Alice looks in the car. She sees the teddy bear on the back seat. Georges points it out to her.

For you!

Alice's expression turns sombre.

ALICE
He won't come . . . That's it, he won't come.

Georges's expression darkens too, as he witnesses Alice's disappointment.

They hear people shouting inside the house.

INT. JULIE'S SITTING-ROOM. DAY

Julie goes upstairs. Harry grabs her by the feet. She falls. He pulls her down by her feet. She screams and clings on to the banisters. Julie's mother tugs at Harry's collar.

Georges bursts in. He sees what is going on and jumps on Harry.

Georges takes Harry by the waist. Julie yells. Harry tries to break free but Georges is stronger than he is. Georges pulls him towards the door.

HARRY

Georges! Let go of me!

GEORGES

My mate Harry! Come!

HARRY

Let go!

GEORGES

Calm down, Harry. Quiet. My mate.

He drags him to the door. A voice stops them in their tracks.

ALICE

Daddy?

Alice is at the door. She sees her father, with Georges holding him by the waist. Everyone stops moving and looks at her. Juliette takes Alice's hand. Harry is embarrassed. Georges does not let go of him.

HARRY

I . . . I came to . . . give you your birthday present.

Alice looks round the chaos in the sitting-room, sees her mother in tears, the broken crockery, her father's distress.

ALICE

I know. Thanks.

Silence. Georges releases Harry.

Well, you've done what you came to do.

Harry stares at Alice. He is not sure he has understood what she is saying. She looks to Georges.

Thank you.

She gives Georges a smile, then turns to her father.

Goodbye, then.

Goodbye.

Alice gently closes the door behind him.

EXT. JULIE'S MOTHER'S STREET. DAY

Harry stares at the door. Georges drags him towards the car. Harry sits on the bonnet and starts to cry. His lips shake. Georges takes him in his arms and rocks him like a baby. Harry buries his face in Georges's shoulder. Georges strokes his neck. Harry sobs. Georges takes a handkerchief out of his pocket and wipes Harry's nose.

GEORGES

My mate Harry.

HARRY

My mate Georges.

Georges pinches Harry's nose, to get a laugh out of him.

GEORGES

Putt-putt. Ha ha.

Harry can't laugh. Georges pulls the corners of his mouth up with his fingers.

Smile, Harry.

Georges gives him an ugly grin.

Smile. Like this. Ha ha.

He makes funny faces.

EXT. SEA-DYKE. CAMPSITE AND FUNFAIR. DAY

Harry is on a swing. Georges is pushing him. They are on the edge of a campsite, beside the car and not far from the apartment blocks.

GEORGES

Still sad?

Georges goes to the entrance of the funfair. The attractions are covered in tarpaulins. The funfair is shut. Georges shakes the gates.

Open up! For my mate Harry! OPEN UP!

Nothing moves. Harry lies prostrate, leaning against the side of his car. Georges sits him in the passenger seat and gets in behind the wheel. He turns the key. The engine turns over. Harry wakes up.

HARRY

Hey! No.

GEORGES

Ha ha. Good joke.

EXT. ROAD. DAY

The car drives along beside the river.

GEORGES
(*off-screen*)
Listen, Harry, good joke. Two madmen are painting this ceiling, and one of them says to the other . . .

HARRY
(*off-screen*)
. . . Hold on to the ladder, I'm taking away the brush.

GEORGES
(*off-screen*)
Yes . . .

They burst out laughing.

EXT. WOOD. DAY

The car is parked on the outskirts of a wood. Georges removes Harry's shoes and socks. He pulls Harry up. Harry walks barefoot on the grass.

GEORGES

Does it tickle?

Harry puts his feet gingerly on the grass and closes his eyes so he can feel the tingle.

Harry and Georges, lying on the ground, watching ants transporting dry blades of grass.

Georges puts Harry up against a tree trunk. Harry closes his eyes. Move up the trunk . . . between the branches . . . along the leaves . . . Harry 'feels' the tree, his eyes closed.

Harry and Georges lying on the grass, in opposite directions. The sun is shining. Their heads touch. Georges looks up at the way the branches of a tree stand out against the sky. He closes one eye then the other. The branches jump slightly. Harry does the same thing. Shadows dance across their faces. Sun diffused through the leaves.

> HARRY

We have to go.

> GEORGES

One minute.

Harry looks at his watch.

> HARRY

OK. One minute. From now.

They remain lying beside each other. They watch the clouds in the sky. From time to time, Georges points out a shape in the clouds. The minute passes by – in real time. They do not move. They seem content.

This takes time. A real minute. Nothing moves.

Then Harry looks at his watch.

Slowly.

That's it.

Georges turns to Harry with a smile.

> GEORGES

That was a beautiful minute. It was ours, it was.

INT. HOTEL ROOM. DAY

Harry and Georges walk into a luxurious, twin-bedded hotel room. Georges is fascinated to switch the lights on and off. He presses a button on the remote control and the TV set flashes. The bellboy waits by the door with the suitcase. Georges goes to take it off him. The bellboy holds

out his hand. Georges shakes it. The bellboy keeps his hand extended.
Georges stares at him, then kisses him on the cheek and closes the door.

INT. HOTEL ROOM. NIGHT

Georges is in his pyjamas. He stands opposite Harry and makes a face
that resembles a smile.

> GEORGES

Well brushed?

Harry nods yes. Georges slips under the bedclothes.

Sing.

Harry switches the lights out. He sits on the edge of the bed. Georges
closes his eyes. Harry gives it a go. His voice sounds shaky.

> HARRY
> (*singing*)
> *Au clair de la lune, mon ami Pierrot,*
> *Prête moi ta plume pour écrire un mot,*
> *Ma chandelle est morte . . .*[1]

Harry stops. He's forgotten the rest.

> GEORGES
> *. . . je n'ai plus de feu . . .*
> (The fire is out . . .)

> HARRY
> *Je n'ai plus de feu . . .*
> *Va chez . . . la voisine . . .*[2]

> GEORGES
> *Ouvre-moi ta porte . . .*[3]

1 By the light of the moon, my friend Pierrot,
Lend me your pen so I can write,
my candle's run out . . .
2 The fire is out . . .
Go to the neighbours next door . . .
3 Open up the door . . .

Ouvre-moi ta porte, pour l'amour de Dieu.[1]

Georges shuts his eyes. Harry falls silent. He strokes Georges's head and goes to sleep in the other bed.

GEORGES

My mate Harry . . .

INT. HOTEL ROOM. NIGHT

Harry is asleep. The TV is on. The sound is off. On the screen, Luis Mariano looking round the room. His image gives way to a commercial break. Georges turns over. His arm goes out and his hand touches the floor. Sound of scratching . . .

We go down through the floor . . .

INT. RAFTERS. NIGHT

In the dusty space between the rafters, a Mouse makes its way . . . up . . . and along a pipe . . .

INT. HOTEL ROOM. NIGHT

The Mouse emerges from a small hole and moves across the floor. There is a cheese commercial on TV . . . The Mouse watches with interest . . . It comes towards Georges, pauses, opens its mouth.

MOUSE

Hey! Psssst!

Georges opens his eyes. He sees the mouse.

It's me. Luis!

GEORGES

Luis Mariano?

MOUSE

I'm in disguise so they don't recognize me. Incognito.

---

1 Open up the door, for the love of God.

He sings.

> *Maman, c'est toi la plus belle du monde,*
> *Aucune à la ronde n'est plus jolie que toi . . .*

Georges is delighted. In the background, the curtains sway in time.
Georges's trousers start to dance, Georges's shoes beat time. Suddenly,
the Mouse vanishes in a puff of smoke. The smoke disperses: the Mouse
has become an ostrich. It struts around the bed, in time. The room seems
larger than before. Georges smiles and rubs his eyes. Doves come to rest
on the window-ledge. The window is open.

The ostrich struts forward and . . . Luis Mariano in person comes and
sits on the edge of Georges's bed, dressed in a sparkling Mexican
costume. He finishes a verse of his song and gives a toothy smile.
Georges smiles too. Harry is still asleep.

GEORGES

Luis!

LUIS MARIANO

Georges!

GEORGES

You've got fatter.

LUIS MARIANO

Too much chocolate.

Wing-beat. A dove comes to rest on Georges's shoulder. Another lands
on his hand. Another on his shoulder. Doves cling on to his pyjamas
and lift him up. Georges flies through the room, round and round above
the bed. Luis sings.

In the background, Georges sees his Mum seated at a small round table.
On the table: a teapot and a steaming cup of tea. She sips at the tea
and nibbles an orange. Beside her is Georges's dog, the one that Harry
ran over. Georges's Mum strokes the dog's head.

The doves bring Georges down onto the bed. He smiles at his Mum.

MUM

How's my little boy?

LUIS MARIANO
Your mum told me you've found a new friend.

Georges indicates Harry's sleeping form.

GEORGES
My mate Harry. I've got a friend.

MUM
I'm happy for you.

LUIS MARIANO
He seems nice.

GEORGES
I'm going to live at Harry's. Beautiful house with TV.

MUM
And what about him? Does he agree?

GEORGES
Yes, he says yes. He's Georges's mate.

MUM
Have you asked him?

Georges lowers his eyes.

MUM

You have to look life in the face, Georges.

LUIS MARIANO

I'm not reality.

GEORGES

Me live with Harry and then me find wife and make marriage.

MUM

Not so fast, Georges. Harry is not ready for you. He's got a life of his own.

Georges seems not to understand.

You are the nicest person in the world. You can do whatever you want. Look. Give me your hand.

Georges reaches out. His mother puts her orange down on the table. Gently, the orange starts to move. It rolls all the way into Georges's hand. He closes his fingers over the orange.

You are an angel, my angel. You are love on earth. There's nothing in you that isn't made of love. But not everyone is like you, darling. You're different.

GEORGES

Me like to be like everyone else.

He hides his eyes. When he opens them, his Mum has gone. So has Luis Mariano. The teacup has gone. On the table, there is the faintest trace of a circular stain where the teapot was . . . Gradually, the circle evaporates and vanishes.

Georges slips into Harry's bed.

My mate . . .

INT. HOTEL ROOM. MORNING

CHEF

Mix the chocolate carefully with the egg-white, making sure you don't break the froth . . .

The chef's smiling face on TV. Georges's elbow knocks Harry's face. Harry opens his eyes. Daylight. The sound of the TV fills the room. Georges is sitting on the bed watching his favourite cookery programme. He copies the chef's gestures, without realizing that every time he moves he gives Harry a knock.

INT. HOTEL BATHROOM. MORNING

Georges stands at the mirror. His cheeks are covered in shaving foam. Harry is shaving him with care. The blade slides gently over his cheeks. Georges is delighted. He examines himself in the mirror.

GEORGES

Georges.

Then Harry shaves himself. He looks at himself in the mirror. A good long look, as though he isn't sure who he is.

HARRY

Harry.

EXT. COUNTRY ROAD. DAY

Harry and Georges driving along a country road.

Where are we going?

Harry does not reply. He seems worried.

Harry?

Harry says nothing.

EXT. INSTITUTE. DAY

The car appears at the gates. It goes up the drive. Georges recognizes the drive . . . the building. He stares at Harry, astonished. Then he turns back to look at the institute.

Georges seems incredibly disappointed. Harry comes to a stop by the building. The patients stare from the windows. Harry and Georges wait for a moment, without speaking. Harry is embarrassed. Georges's hand feels for Harry's hand. He holds it tight.

They get out of the car. Georges takes Harry in his arms.

                          HARRY
I'm sorry, I can't . . . I can't even look after my own children.

Harry takes the teddy bear out of the back of the car and gives it to Georges. Georges's friends form a circle around them. We recognize the same characters as at the beginning: Nathalie, Fernand, Yvan, Jacques, Jean . . . Nathalie takes Georges by the hand.

                          GEORGES
This is my friend Harry. He's got problems.

They draw close around Harry, touch him, stare at him. Harry is somewhat frightened. He pushes his way through to his car and takes refuge.

Harry starts the engine. In the rear-view mirror, he sees Georges shrinking in the distance.
        FADE TO BLACK.

INT. HARRY'S BEDROOM. DAY

The alarm clock moves to 7.30. The radio comes on.

It is 7.30 a.m. and the outside temperature is . . . (*continues*)

INT. HARRY'S KITCHEN. DAY

A slice of toast jumps out of the toaster.

INT. HARRY'S BATHROOM. DAY

The toothbrush drops back into the glass. Harry looks at himself in the mirror glumly.

INT. MEETING-ROOM. DAY

Harry goes into a meeting-room and sits down. A few people turn towards him. Bruno is standing beside the director, talking to a client.

BRUNO
Eighty per cent of our customers' decisions are based on their emotional reactions, their first impressions, their intuition. They are not logical. Don't forget, your image is your employees' image. How they behave towards the client. How they talk to them. What they wear. How they look. How they smile. Nothing should be left to chance.

Harry watches him. Bruno has copied Harry's tone, his conviction. He's a carbon copy of Harry a few days earlier. The client listens attentively. Harry, on the other hand, does not seem interested. His gaze turns to the window. A ladybird is climbing up the glass.

HARRY
Hello . . . a ladybird.

Everyone falls silent. They turn and stare at Harry.

INT. HARRY'S OFFICE. DAY

Harry is at his desk. He is shredding his notes. The bin is overflowing. Harry stares straight ahead without blinking. A Cleaning Lady appears with a cart. Harry does not move. She approaches.

CLEANING LADY
Is everything all right?

85

Harry does not react.

INT. HARRY'S GARAGE. NIGHT

The automatic door shuts as Harry's car enters the garage. Harry remains at the wheel of his car, in the dark.

INT. HARRY'S LIVING ROOM. NIGHT

The TV set is on but there's nothing but the test card, then snow. In the dark, Harry dials a number.

JULIE'S VOICE

Hello?

Harry says nothing.

Hello?

Silence.

Harry? . . . Is that you? . . .

Harry says nothing. He opens his mouth, but no sound emerges.

Leave me alone, Harry . . . I beg you . . . You frighten me.

She hangs up.

Harry does not move. He is pensive.

HARRY

My mate Georges.

INT. SPECIAL WORKSHOP. DAY

Racket. Machines working. A workshop. A packaging line. One of the Down's syndrome patients, Alain, drives a forklift truck. Boxes pass by in front of Georges on a conveyor belt. Georges wears blue overalls. The others are all around him.

Georges is with a Social Worker.

SOCIAL WORKER

Look. This is how it works.

86

The Social Worker scratches his nose. He takes some small boxes and places them inside a larger box. He glances at Georges. Georges scratches his nose, then puts a small box inside a larger one. The Social Worker watches him in puzzlement, then moves off. Beside him is Yvan. Pierre is on the other side.

YVAN

Femme, toi si belle,
Toi si parfaite sous la tonnelle,
Je t'aime de tant d'amour
Que j'en rêve le jour.[1]

PIERRE

Do you know Nathalie is leaving?

GEORGES

What?

PIERRE

She's going to stay with her parents.

Pierre hands him a box which is full. Georges sets about emptying it, removing the boxes. Pierre, on the contrary, refills. The Social Worker rushes over.

SOCIAL WORKER
(*to Georges*)

Fill the boxes! Don't empty them!

Georges puts on a foolish expression, tongue hanging out. The Social Worker looks at him with despair.

Never mind. You can go.

Georges takes his apron off. He proudly walks across the workshop.

GEORGES

Me no work!

1 Lady, so lovely,
 so perfect in your bower,
 such is the love I love you
 that all day long I dream of it.

The other patients burst out laughing, but hide their faces as they do so.
Jean starts emptying boxes instead of filling them.

INT. CORRIDOR AND NATHALIE'S ROOM. DAY

Georges pushes Nathalie's door ajar and peeks through the crack. He
sees a suitcase on the bed. A woman social worker is emptying a
cupboard and filling the suitcase. One by one Nathalie removes the
pictures tacked to the wall: portraits of French rock star Johnny
Halliday and photos of horses. Georges looks worried.

INT. GEORGES'S ROOM. EVENING

Georges is at his window. He sees Nathalie's parents below. Nathalie is
wearing a coat. She waits beside the car. Her parents load her case into
the boot. Nathalie spies Georges at the window and waves goodbye.
Georges sees her climb into the car. The car drives off in a cloud of dust.

INT. GEORGES'S ROOM. NIGHT

Georges is lying on his bed. He opens his eyes.

GEORGES
My mate Harry . . .

EXT. HARRY'S NEIGHBOUR'S GARDEN. NIGHT

Harry creeps up to his next-door neighbour's pool. He puts a foot on the
surface of the water. He does not sink in. He walks on the water,
looking debonair.

FADE TO BLACK.

INT. AUDITORIUM. DAY

'Delta Bank' above the stage. Technicians set up a speaker's platform.
Mike tests.

INT. GEORGES'S ROOM. DAY

Georges is sitting on his bed. He stares into the hollow of his hand.
Barely legible, the number 14 is written there. Then Georges glances at a
calendar on the wall. The calendar says today is the 14th.

In the corridor, the patients are getting ready, putting their coats on. Georges puts his coat on and joins them.

INT. MUSEUM. DAY

A room in the museum. Classical canvases on the wall. Patients from the institute pass by, looking at the pictures. They seem bored. Georges is among them, worrying about something. The Social Worker is at the head of the group, commenting on the pictures. Georges signals to some of his friends that they should follow him. Almost everyone leaves the room. The Social Worker turns round. There are just two people in the room with him. The others have vanished.

SOCIAL WORKER

Hey!

INT. SHOPPING CENTRE. DAY

The gang moves quickly through a shopping centre, laughing. Lights, garlands, neon signs. Magnificent, luxurious displays, mannequins, beautiful clothes, household appliances . . . They look lovingly at the various stalls, including people selling balloons.

INT. CAR SHOWROOM. DAY

Georges and his friends enter a car showroom and disperse among the various cars. They stare at and feel the cars. Other customers are somewhat intrigued by their behaviour. A salesman speaks to Jacques.

SALESMAN

Please don't touch.

All smiling, Georges, Jacques, Jean, Pierre and Guy approach one of the salesmen sitting at a desk. Panic in his eyes.

GEORGES
(to Pierre)

You talk to him, you know how to.

PIERRE

We're a small group of friends and we'd like to borrow a car to go to the seaside.

89

The Salesman can't think of anything to say.

> GEORGES
> (*to Philippe*)
> He doesn't understand. You try.

> PHILIPPE
> We're expected at a little girl's birthday party but first we have
> to pick up a friend . . .

> GEORGES
> Harry . . .

> PHILIPPE
> Harry, and another friend of ours, a girl, as well . . .

> GEORGES
> Nathalie . . .

> PHILIPPE
> Nathalie. So we need the use of a car.

> GEORGES
> Ask politely.

> PHILIPPE
> Politely.

> GUY
> We'd like a car.

> SALESMAN
> Errr . . . and who's going to drive it?

*They all point to Alain (the driver of the forklift truck in the workshop).
Alain smiles proudly.*

> Just a moment . . . Boss!

*The Manager happens to be displaying a six-seat micro-bus to a
customer. Pierre comes up to them. The Manager puts the key in the
ignition to show how the electric roof works. Pierre gestures to the others.
The Salesman is also making desperate signals to his Manager.*

MANAGER

(*to customer*)

Just a moment, please.

The Manager goes over to his Salesman and passes the gang moving towards the micro-bus. They climb inside and feel the softness of the seats. The Manager runs up, furious, followed by the Salesman. At the sight of him, the gang take fright and shut themselves in the bus. Georges locks his door. All the other doors lock automatically. The Manager and the Salesman hammer at the windscreen and bang on the doors. Through the glass, their shouting is audible. Their hands press against the windscreen. The gang do not know what to do. Vincent and Isabelle start yelling with fear. Alain sees the key in the ignition and turns it. The engine starts. The Manager and his Salesmen look thunderstruck. Alain presses the accelerator down to the floor. The wheels skid on the carpet. The micro-bus squeals across the showroom. It goes through the plate-glass window, which shatters.

INT. SHOPPING CENTRE. DAY

The bus drives at top speed through the shopping centre. Screams. Panic. People move out of the way, throwing themselves aside. The bus knocks over promotional stands. A Security Officer pulls out a gun as he sees the micro-bus pass. Alain shuts his eyes and puts his foot down. The gang shriek and put their hands over their eyes. Nicolas lowers his window and puts his arm out. He catches hold of a bunch of multicoloured balloons. The micro-bus shoots through the shopping centre, balloons streaming out behind.

EXT. CITY STREET. DAY

The micro-bus bursts out into a street, with a promotional stand caught on its front bumper. It squeals round a corner and disappears off in the distance. The Security Officer runs up. He aims at the vehicle, but it's too late.

EXT. OFFICE BLOCK. DAY

The micro-bus stops at the foot of Harry's office block. Jean has a map on his knees. They all look up at the office block.

INT. AUDITORIUM. DAY

A vast auditorium filled with businessmen. On the platform, the Director surrounded by his team. On one side, Harry is speaking into the microphone.

HARRY

Borders are coming down. Banks . . .

Harry looks at his audience. They are listening with care. He glances at his notes.

. . . sell services increasingly similar from one country to another. They must be able to compete internationally.

A few moments' silence. Harry's eyes sweep round the audience. He is having difficulty pulling his thoughts together.

. . . internationally or be swallowed up: that is the choice which . . .

Another pause. People stare at him with concern.

. . . the choice which . . .

Harry falls silent. A glacial hush fills the room. Someone coughs. No one moves. Harry examines the audience. Sound of feedback in his mike. The doors at the back of the room open. Silhouettes clutching balloons tied on the ends of bits of string come into the auditorium. Georges and his friends have arrived. They spread out through the audience. Jacques disrupts the silence by making a bugle sound. People turn round. They want to know what is going on.

GEORGES

My mate Harry!

HARRY

My mate Georges!

Georges shows him the palm of his hand, marked '14'.

EXT. OFFICE-BLOCK ROOF. DAY

Crates of fireworks pass from hand to hand.

INT. OFFICE-BLOCK FIRE STAIRS. DAY

Harry, Georges and the gang tumble down the stairs, carrying the crates.

EXT. ROAD. DAY

The micro-bus zigzags down a country road. Firework crates are loaded in the back. Harry and Georges are surrounded by the other members of the gang. Jean chats to Harry. The others watch the countryside go by, delighted. Pierre plays a tune on his trombone.

INT. HARRY'S SITTING-ROOM. DAY

The TV is on in Harry's sitting-room. It shows pictures of the ruined shopping centre. The showroom Manager is being interviewed. There are policemen in the background. The sound is off.

EXT. NATHALIE'S HOUSE. DAY

By the stables, a girl in riding clothes gets on to a horse. This is Nathalie.

EXT. NATHALIE'S STREET. DAY

*The micro-bus stops by a park. Harry and the gang look over the hedge.
They see an enormous avenue set in a field.*

EXT. NATHALIE'S HOUSE. DAY

*Nathalie trots through the field. From the far side of a rise, the roof of
the micro-bus slowly emerges. Harry is at the wheel.*

EXT. MONGOLIAN STEPPE. DAY

*Georges is on horseback, dressed as a Mongol prince. The gang are
behind him, dressed as Mongol knights, galloping across the plains . . .*

*Opposite, Nathalie on horseback, dressed as a Mongolian princess. She
watches them ride towards her. The gang comes to a halt when they reach
her. She looks into Georges's eyes. He returns her look. They smile . . .*

EXT. NATHALIE'S HOUSE. DAY

*Nathalie's horse returns to the stable without its rider. The micro-bus
vanishes at the far end of the field.*

EXT. ROAD. DAY

*Harry is driving. Georges and Nathalie are side by side. Nathalie's
hand grazes Georges's. Their little fingers touch. They do not move.
Georges looks out. He is exploding with inner joy. The micro-bus
disappears up the road . . .*

EXT. CARAVAN SITE AND FUNFAIR. NIGHT

*The micro-bus drives across the deserted caravan site and reaches the
seashore. Georges, Harry and the gang stare out to sea, thinking how
beautiful it is. The funfair is right ahead of them, covered in tarpaulins
and all locked up. A big wheel sits motionless in the sky. Beyond some
sand-dunes, the apartment blocks.*

*They get out of the bus. Fernand, who is big and strong, grabs the gates
and yanks the posts up as hard as he can. They come out of the ground
and the gates collapse. Laughter and applause. Madly excited, they run
into the fair and pull all the tarpaulins off.*

Harry goes into the phone booth beside the campsite. He dials a number.

INT. JULIE'S HOUSE. NIGHT

Darkness. On a table, the remains of a birthday cake. The phone rings.

EXT. FUNFAIR AND CARAVAN SITE. NIGHT

Harry hangs up. Harry opens the back of the micro-bus and pulls the firework crates on to the sand.

Using a lighter, Dominique peers at a fusebox. He pulls at the mains switch. Lights go on all over the place. The sound of an electric organ. The funfair lights up. The merry-go-round is all decked out in garlands of light. Dominique yells in triumph.

Some of the others appear out of a shed, carrying bottles of beer. They laugh and dance.

They clamber up on to wooden horses. Georges finds a switch and the merry-go-round starts to turn. The horses go round beneath the big wheel, which is all lit up. Everyone is laughing. Standing by the main switches, Georges looks on radiantly happy. Nathalie comes up beside him.

NATHALIE
I'm not in love with Johnny Halliday now, you know.

Georges smiles. They go off, leaving the switches to themselves.

INT. CARAVAN. NIGHT

The door to one of the caravans has been forced open. Georges and Nathalie are inside in the dark, lying on a bed, pressed against one another. They are looking into each other's eyes. Gently, Georges undoes Nathalie's collar. He brings her back forwards and tries to unfasten her bra. She doesn't know what to make of this and moves a fraction.

NATHALIE
We can't. It's not allowed.

Georges pauses. He looks her in the eye.

GEORGES

What can't we?

NATHALIE

You know . . . make love.

GEORGES

Who says?

NATHALIE

My daddy says.

GEORGES

Your daddy does it. Doesn't he?

NATHALIE

Yes, but that's different . . . He's normal. He goes to work, he's a director, he's got a car and everything.

GEORGES

I don't want to make love to a director.

Nathalie laughs. Georges comes close to her. She pretends that the electric light outside the window is too strong and hides her eyes. Georges gets up and closes the blind. The caravan grows darker. Just as Georges is about to lie down again, the blind suddenly rolls up. Georges sighs, gets up again, pulls the blind down. He lets go of it very gently, backs towards the bed and, just as he is about to turn to Nathalie, the blind goes up again with a bang. Georges sighs deeply . . . He returns to the blind, carefully brings it down and jams it down with a chair . . . It stays in place. He takes Nathalie in his arms. The blind comes away from the wall and crashes down. Nathalie bursts out laughing. So does Georges.

EXT. FUNFAIR. NIGHT

The others on the merry-go-round signal it's time to stop. There's no one at the switches. They want to get down. They've had enough. One of them is feeling unwell.

FERNAND

GEORGES! . . . Where is he?

96

INT. CARAVAN. NIGHT

Georges's T-shirt is over the window. Georges and Nathalie are on the bed, naked, holding each other tight and calm. They breathe deeply and stare up dreamily at the ceiling. The sound of firework rockets wakes them up. Georges is excited. He gets up.

EXT. BEACH. NIGHT

Georges runs across the beach, doing up his trousers as he goes. He joins Harry. They take rockets out and plant them in the sand. They are both excited. They run around laughing. Harry lights flares . . . Harry and Georges run from one rocket to another, lighting the fuses. Rockets go off all over the place, whistling. Sprays of colour light up the sky . . . Harry runs, mad for joy. Great fire blossoms spray up everywhere . . . on the beach, above the apartment blocks, between the houses, just outside people's windows. Lights go on. People appear at the windows.

EXT. FUNFAIR. NIGHT

The gang enjoys the firework display.

EXT. JULIE'S HOUSE. NIGHT

Alice appears in the window of her house. Juliette joins her. Rockets go off all around them. They watch the sprays of colour in amazement. Julie comes and joins them.

EXT. BEACH. NIGHT

Harry runs up and down the beach, from one rocket to another. He pauses for breath and looks towards the house . . .

EXT. JULIE'S HOUSE. NIGHT

The girls are staring at him.

EXT. BEACH. NIGHT

He sees them looking at him.

A police siren in the distance. Georges starts to run towards the funfair. Harry follows.

Harry and Georges run down the dunes and in between the caravans. About ten police cars surround the funfair, their roof lights turning. There is an ambulance. Georges's friends are still trapped on the merry-go-round. They are no longer laughing but waiting, tired, for someone to come and rescue them.

Nathalie hides behind a caravan. Georges comes and finds her. He takes her by the hand.

The policemen gather the gang together. The music comes to a halt. The big wheel stops turning. Everyone climbs down off the merry-go-round. Nathalie's parents push their way through the policemen. Her father calls out:

> NATHALIE'S FATHER
>
> Nathalie!

Near the caravan, Nathalie starts. She looks at Georges, who hides beside her.

> Nathalie!

Nathalie lets go of Georges's hand. She comes out of their hiding place.

> NATHALIE
>
> Daddy . . .

Nathalie's mother wants to run to her daughter, but her husband prevents her from doing so.

> NATHALIE'S FATHER
>
> Come here, Nathalie.

Nathalie does not move. She glances towards Georges.

> Come.

Nathalie walks towards her parents, head down. Her mother takes her in her arms. Her father strokes her head. Nathalie seems submissive.

> It's all over . . . it's all over . . .

Hiding behind the caravan, Georges closes his eyes. He runs towards the dunes. Harry runs after him.

EXT. DUNES. NIGHT

Georges runs like mad through the dunes, yelling. Harry runs after him.

EXT. SEASIDE RESORT. NIGHT

Harry and Georges walk down the pavement. The metal shutter of a TV shop is lowered but the screens are visible beyond, switched on. Georges goes up to the screen. By means of a small camera, one of the screens shows him his own image. Georges watches carefully. He shifts his head to the left, his head in the image shifts to the left . . . He raises his arm, the arm in the image is raised. Then he starts to talk.

> GEORGES
> Ladies and gentlemen of the audience . . . me Georges. Me sad. Please tell my mum to come and fetch me.

On the other screens a silent pop promo appears. Georges copies the singer's movement in perfect sync. His image appears in the middle of the other screens. Harry tries to drag him away but Georges won't have it.

> Me have fun.

He dances on the deserted pavement, wilder and wilder. Harry waits on a bench. A police siren goes off in the distance.

EXT. STREET. NIGHT

Deafening music. Harry and Georges pass by a discotheque. From inside, sound of voices, laughter. Georges goes in. Harry follows him.

INT. DISCO. NIGHT

A crowd on the dance floor, shaking and sweating. Georges pushes his way in and starts to dance. He's having fun, working out.

Harry sits and waits by the exit. Georges goes by the bar and takes a beer without paying for it. A customer watches his beer disappear. Georges empties it at one go. The beer trickles down his mouth, into his neck. Georges thrusts himself back on to the dance floor.

A slower song. Couples form, cling to each other. Boys ask girls to dance. Georges comes to a girl and holds his hand out to her. She looks away. Georges does not move. He stays with his hand out. Another boy asks the girl to dance and she hurriedly accepts. Georges watches her go by, amazed.

He crosses the dance floor. Couples dance clutching each other. One girl dances alone, her eyes closed, sensuous. Georges stands right in front of her. She goes on dancing. Georges tries to put his arms around her. She fights him off. Other couples stop dancing. Everyone stares at Georges. Georges takes a step towards the girl. She looks horrified. He seems to be begging her. She runs off. The barman takes the phone off the hook and dials a number. Harry pushes through the crowd. He picks Georges up off the floor, where he is in tears. He takes him in his arms. It is as if he were picking up a corpse, riven by silent sobs, like a pietà. People start dancing again. Harry goes through the crowd carrying Georges. The crowd parts. They leave.

EXT. STREET. NIGHT

Harry moves away from the disco carrying Georges in his arms. A police siren screams somewhere. In the background (out of focus) a flashing blue light stops outside the disco. Harry and Georges turn the corner.

EXT. TOWN SQUARE. NIGHT

Georges can hardly walk. Harry hugs him. He tries to get him to dance. Georges holds on to him tight. Harry gets Georges to dance from one foot to the other by holding him up. Georges is in tears.

GEORGES

Me want to go back to Mum.

Pause.

Me not quite like other people.

HARRY

That's true. You are better than others.

Georges releases himself from Harry's embrace and goes to sit on a bench. Harry sits next to him. Georges examines his reflection in Harry's eyes.

> GEORGES

In Harry's eyes, I can see Georges.

> HARRY

What can I do, Georges?

> GEORGES

Harry has children. Georges is just another problem for Harry.

> HARRY

That isn't true.

He embraces Georges.

> GEORGES

Me would like to be with my mum.

EXT. SQUARE. NIGHT

Harry and Georges are asleep on the bench in each other's arms. Georges wakes and gets up slowly, without disturbing Harry. Georges moves off a few steps. He stops by a tree and presses his forehead against the tree.

GEORGES

Mum . . .

His mother's hand strokes the back of his neck . . . and he is no longer leaning against the tree but against his mother's shoulder.

MUM

My darling little one . . .

GEORGES

Mum, me want to go with you.

MUM

That isn't possible, my love. I am dead.

GEORGES

Me want to go with you. Things aren't working out for Georges here.

MUM

You have to grow up and be a big boy.

GEORGES

Me don't want to be a big boy. Me want to go with you.

MUM

I'm a long way away, Georges. I'm in heaven.

Georges buries himself in her breast.

You are the best thing that happened in my life, Georges. You are the most beautiful present heaven ever gave me. I loved you from the moment I set eyes on you and I've never stopped loving you.

Georges opens his eyes. He is no longer resting against his mother but against a tree trunk. He shuts his eyes again, as though in pain.

GEORGES

Mum . . .

Georges raises his eyes. He looks up into the sky above. Clouds dance before the moon.

Georges strokes Harry's hair. He takes Harry's wallet out and removes the picture of his children, which he places in Harry's hand. Then Georges leaves.

EXT. SQUARE. DAWN

Day breaks. Harry opens his eyes. He sees the picture of his children in his hand. He looks around.

HARRY

Georges?

Harry runs around the square, shouting out loud.

GEORGES!

He runs in one direction, then another. The streets are deserted, except for a refuse truck. Harry stops in the middle of the square. He is alone.

Harry want Georges.

EXT. JULIE'S HOUSE. DAY

Harry is tired and unshaven, standing across the road from Julie's house without moving.

A curtain opens. Alice's face appears. They look at each other. A moment later, Alice opens the front door. She almost smiles. Juliette appears beside her. Harry crosses the street. The girls run into his arms. Harry falls to his knees and hugs them.

ALICE AND JULIETTE

Daddy!

Julie appears in the doorway. They exchange a look.

Harry hugs his children. In the end, Julie speaks.

JULIE

It was a lovely firework show.

Smiles.

At the end of the street, someone is watching them: Georges. After a while, he moves off.

EXT. OFFICE BLOCK. DAY

The city, seen from an office block.

EXT. OFFICE-BLOCK STREET. DAY

In the window of the same chocolate shop, a huge, heart-shaped box of chocolates tied with ribbon.

Georges takes his piggy bank out of his jacket pocket. He smashes it against the edge of the pavement. A few coins and crumpled notes scatter on the ground. Georges picks them up. He enters the shop.

EXT. OFFICE-BLOCK STREET. DAY

Georges is at the foot of the office block, carrying a box of chocolates. He looks up at the sky, the clouds.

INT. OFFICE BLOCK FIRE-ESCAPE. DAY

Georges climbs up the fire-escape.

EXT. OFFICE BLOCK ROOF AND WINDOWS. DAY

Georges opens the door on the roof and looks up at the sky. He is at the top of the building, very high up in the sky, surrounded by clouds. The city is spread beneath him.

He sits down with the box of chocolates in his lap. He examines the chocolates. He lets his hand wander over them, choosing one. He puts it in his mouth, chews it and savours it. He takes another . . . then another. The clouds shift above him . . . His head starts to turn.

> GEORGES
> (*murmuring*)

Mum . . .

Luis Mariano's song sounds. Georges mouths the words . . .

> Maman, c'est toi la plus belle du monde,
> Aucune autre à la ronde N'est plus jolie.

The box of chocolates slides empty to the ground. Georges takes a few uncertain steps. He falls over the edge of the roof.

The floors pass by him in slow motion . . . Georges watches the windows go by . . . People working in their offices. No one notices him.

In passing, we see a secretary typing . . . a man on the phone . . .

The ground approaches. Grass surrounded by a border. The grass comes closer. A ladybird on a blade of grass. Blackness.

Blades of grass in front of Georges's face as he lies in the grass. A ladybird on the tip of a blade of grass. She spreads her wings and flies away. We rise above Georges . . .

Luis Mariano's song starts up again, sung by the various characters Georges has encountered . . .

EXT. GEORGES'S SISTER'S HOUSE, DAY

His sister in a dressing-gown . . .

SISTER
(*singing*)
Tu as pour moi, Avoue que c'est étrange[1]

---

1 To me you seem to have, admit it's strange . . .

EXT. CAR SHOWROOM. DAY

The Manager of the car showroom, in front of his shattered window . . .

> MANAGER
> *Le visage d'un ange du paradis.*[1]

INT. SHOESHOP. DAY

The Sales assistant . . .

> SALES ASSISTANT
> *Dans tous mes voyages j'ai vu des paysages . . .*[2]

EXT. CITY STREET. DAY

The Policeman, gun in hand . . .

> POLICEMAN
> *Mais rien ne vaut l'image de tes beaux cheveux gris.*[3]

EXT. FUNFAIR. DAY

Nathalie between her parents . . .

> NATHALIE
> *C'est toi, Maman, la plus belle du monde . . .*[4]

INT. HOTEL ROOM. NIGHT

The little mouse in a ring of light . . .

> WHITE MOUSE
> *Et ma joie est profonde lorsqu'à mon bras . . .*[5]

EXT. RUE DES CERISIERS. DAY

The Indian Man, outside Mum's house . . .

---

1 An angel's face, from Paradise.
2 In all my travelling I've seen landscapes . . .
3 But nothing beats the sight of your lovely grey hair.
4 Mum, you are the best in the world . . .
5 And I'm so happy when on my arm . . .

INDIAN MAN
Maman, tu mets ton bras . . . [1]

INT. LIVING-ROOM. INSTITUTE. DAY

On TV, a man in a toothpaste commercial, smiling . . .

ACTOR
Maman, c'est toi, la plus belle du monde . . . [2]

INT. HARRY'S SITTING-ROOM. DAY

The cookery programme presenter, wearing a chef's hat . . .

CHEF
Car tant d'amour inonde tes jolies yeux . . . [3]

INT. COFFEE SHOP. DAY

The Waitress . . .

WAITRESS
Pour toi, c'est vrai, je suis malgré mon âge . . . [4]

EXT. OFFICE BLOCK. DAY

Harry is at the foot of the office block, surrounded by Passers-by. They all sing in chorus . . . An ambulance arrives. Two policemen keep the Passers-by at a distance.

PASSERS-BY
Le petit enfant sage des jours heureux. [5]

FADE TO BLACK.

EXT. STREET. TRAFFIC JAM. DAY

A car, identical to Harry's, is stuck behind a refuse truck. The street is jammed. Refuse collectors gather up plastic bags. Honking. The driver

1 You lay your arm, Mum . . .
2 You, Mum, are the best in the world . . .
3 Because so much love fills your lovely eyes . . .
4 For you, it's true, despite my age. I am . . .
5 The good little boy of our happy days.

presses on his horn. We move up towards his face . . . It isn't Harry. A stranger. On the pavement, a man turns round. He is beside the refuse truck, smiling. He gives the finger. This is Harry. He helps the men and – to their surprise – starts handing them the bins. A black refuse collector gives him a slap on the back. They chuckle.

EXT. INSTITUTE GROUNDS. DAY

> HARRY
> (*voice-over*)

In the beginning there was nothing at all. Only music.

Black. Luis Mariano's voice in the distance singing 'Mexico'.

On the first day, he made the sun. He switched on the day and switched out the night . . . Everyone's eyes started to sting.

> FADE UP.

Harry's face, turned towards the sun, smiling. His eyes are closed.

EXT. SEA. DAY

> HARRY
> (*voice-over*)

On the second day, he made water. It was wet. Your feet get wet if you walk in it.

Harry's feet on sand, surrounded by his two children's feet. A wave breaks over the sand and covers their feet in water.

EXT. INSTITUTE GROUNDS. DAY

Harry's hair ruffled by the breeze. He flattens it.

> HARRY
> (*voice-over*)

Then he made the wind. Wind tickles.

A lawnmower passes by. The blades squeal. Harry's hand caresses the grass, followed by his children's hands.

The third day, he made the grass. When you cut it, it screams. It hurts. You have to make it better, say nice things to it.

Julie waves goodbye to her children, who jump up and kiss Harry.

Harry and his children press their faces against a tree, keeping their eyes closed. We move up the trunk, along the bark.

If you touch a tree, you become a tree.

Georges is sitting in a tree, watching the scene and smiling . . .

On the fourth day, he made cows. They blow warm.

EXT. FIELD. DAY

Harry's hand strokes a cow's moist nose.

EXT. FIELD NEAR AIRPORT. DAY

Harry is in the middle of a field. In the distance, a plane takes off. It passes above him.

> HARRY
> (*voice-over*)

On the fifth day, he made aeroplanes. If you don't travel in them, you can watch them overhead.

EXT. INSTITUTE GROUNDS AND SKY. DAY

> HARRY
> (*voice-over*)

On the sixth day, he made people. I prefer kissing women and children, because they don't prickle when you kiss them.

Juliette's cheeks. Harry kisses her. Alice's hand, stroking Harry's hand.

On the seventh day, it was time to rest, so he made the clouds. If you watch them for long enough, you can see all kinds of stories in them.

Harry is lying on a lawn with his children either side of him. He shows them the clouds and tells them a story. The girls burst out laughing.

Harry and his daughters watch a ladybird climbing up a blade of grass . . . They shut their eyes. The ladybird spreads its wings and flies away. We fly off above Harry and his children, above the trees.

Then he wondered whether he had forgotten anything. And on the eighth day, he made Georges. And he realized that that was that.

Georges's smiling face.

Toto the Hero
(or How to Mess Up Your Life
for No Apparent Reason)

MOVIE LESSONS
Jaco Van Dormael in Conversation with Pierre Hodgson
Brussels, January 1992

It was a cold day in January 1992. I arrived in Brussels at about ten
in the morning. The train was late. It was almost snowing. I used
to work here, ten years ago. I hadn't been back. I was struck by the
faces on the Métro – there are more different races (and more
different languages) than anywhere else in Europe. Despite the
skyscraper banality of its Eurobanks and Euro-offices, Brussels
remains a quirky town and a strong one, where the cafés stay open
half the night and even in the mornings they are thick with the
convivial stench of beer and smoke and steaming human beings.

Our conversation was conducted in French. Jaco had given, in
the previous weeks and months, 350 interviews on the subject of
his film. He was wary of sounding stale and he was not willing to
discuss future plans. Consequently, we found ourselves talking
about making films in general, about what works and what
doesn't. And when we found ourselves straying on to ground
covered already by Jaco while promoting *Toto the Hero*, we would
skid to a halt and seek a passage into virgin territory. The result is
a conversation piece necessarily irregular and scrappy in its
construction, but as fresh and as true as we could make it. It aims
to provide an insight into the thoughts of a singularly thoughtful
film-maker.

THE THREE AGES OF FILM: WRITING, SHOOTING, EDITING

In the Beginning . . .

JACO VAN DORMAEL: I start with chaos, with bits and pieces. I
scribble on index cards, then file them away in boxes. That goes
on for months. I write a few scenes, fragments, not much more
than that, shopping for images, characters, scenes. Nothing is
excluded. I go off in lots of different directions, worry about all the
potential avenues, so that when the time comes to narrow the
scope, I have as much raw material as possible. This is not an

efficient way of working. I could first devise an initial structure, then fill it out, which would be quicker. As it is, I am likely to lose my way. I never know whether I'm making any headway, or when a script is definitively finished. But my method does have one great advantage: the story appears to be writing itself. It feels natural, because when I do arrive at some sort of structure, it has been generated by the material from within, and not imposed from without. Structure is what I'm most interested in, more than actual scenes, because the meaning of a film is in its structure, its narrative.

Finding out What a Story is About

JVD: I wrote the first version of *Toto* a long time ago, in 1982. It centred on the children, the adults did not come into it. I didn't like it, so I put it in a drawer. The story only began to grab me when there was a contrast between the different periods of the same characters' lives. I began to think: this is more like it, this confusion between past and present is what life is like. The story was still all over the place, but it did have one big connecting theme: that there is no such thing as fate. Rimbaud said: 'We slip into behaving a little less well than expected; we do things which, on the whole, we would rather not have done; and then, when our lives are finished, it turns out that it is not as we would have wished. And, of course by then it is too late.' That comes from a letter he wrote to his sister when he was thirty, dealing in arms in Abyssinia and about to have his leg amputated. He couldn't see any connection between that Rimbaud and the other one, the young poet of Charleville. I know what he means, I recognize the sensation. He means there is no such thing as fate. And that is why, in the plot of *Toto*, age matters: if we could simultaneously witness ourselves at twenty, at forty, at sixty, we would discover how it is we slip into becoming something other than what we hoped we would be.

When, in *Toto* the old man looks in the mirror and imagines what he was like forty years before, or the middle-aged man looks in the mirror and thinks back to what he was like twenty years earlier, it is the gap, the abyss of years, which matters.

JVD: I need discipline otherwise I just sit and stare out of the window. So I write for three hours a day, every day. I do this five days a week, Monday to Friday. I rest at weekends. That way, things move forward. Sometimes, I sit down to write and I think, 'today I don't know what to write' and sometimes there really is nothing in my brain so I muck around, I write the first thing that comes to me, whatever that may be. Most of the time, the script is off the road, like a broken-down car. I spend half my time under the bonnet, fixing things. My maddest ideas always come to me when things look bleakest. You pull something out of the hat to get things going again. Sometimes, there is only one sentence out of a whole day's work, out of the three pages, which is worth keeping. But then the day is worth it for that one sentence.

PIERRE HODGSON: *And do you ever laugh at what you've written?*

JVD: No. Sometimes I think it's funny, but I can't laugh. Obviously, I am hugely nervous about the way things are going. Nobody likes what they write. Anyway I have this discipline. Every Friday afternoon people come over, friends, and they read whatever I've got to give them. They're all close friends. For *Toto* there was Laurette and Didier who plays Mr Kant (the baddie supermarket owner) and Pascal, who is a friend and a scriptwriter. They all come on Friday afternoons and say: oh yes, that's good; or I see they are laughing, and I draw my conclusions. They are my audience if you like. I need the feedback. That way I am not working in a vacuum. I couldn't work all on my own, it is unbearable over a long period. After two months, you just get depressed. Either that or you are so desperate to finish you rush things. I need a lot of time for a story to fall into shape. I don't know the meaning of inspiration. Routine is all I have.

PH: *Isn't everyone like that?*

JVD: No, there are some people, I know some, who suddenly think of something and write for three days and three nights without a break, drinking lots of coffee. I cannot do that. I never think up an idea for a whole film. If I wrote fifteen pages a day, I'd throw twelve away so I might as well stick to three.

JVD: I was taught screenwriting by Frank Daniel who is from Czechoslovakia. He was head of FAMU, the Prague Film School, until 1968, when he emigrated to the United States. In New York, he opened a film school with Milos Forman called, I think, the Film Institute. Later, he became head of the film department at USC. Every summer for six or seven years, he would come over to Belgium and teach us what questions we ought to be asking about our own scripts, the common sense questions an audience is going to ask: 'What does this character want?', 'Why does he want it?'. He was never prescriptive, but he did make it plain that it was our job to know the answers – which was salutary. Usually, screenwriters avoid asking themselves anything which is going to cause trouble.

PH: *What about structure?*

JVD: He was much stricter about structure. He would make comments like the second act starts too late or this statement has to come earlier.

PH: *Was he an advocate of that American method which says after eight minutes such and such has to happen?*

JVD: Absolutely. That is how I wrote *Toto*. First act ends on page 24; page 68, beginning of the third act; a major explosion at the midpoint; set up and pay off; beats and so on. The system works because it is natural. The audience expects an event – after twenty-six minutes or between the twenty-fifth and the thirtieth minute – which changes the course of the story, and brings in act two, which is the period of conflict. If that event comes too late, the film feels slow, and if it doesn't happen at all, the audience thinks the story is incomprehensible because, from the beginning of time, that is how stories have been told. What we call the American system is only the Eastern European system. When the talkies came, Hollywood imported all these German, French, Eastern European, Hungarian writers and their rules came from Greek theatre. They are the rules of rhetoric. They haven't changed. They've merely been adapted to film. The main narrative issues remain the same.

PH: *How do your three pages a day get transformed into a structured whole?*

JVD: I look to see if any kind of pattern emerges from the raw material. I put huge sheets of paper on the wall and I start to make charts. And when a story begins to emerge, I show it to my collaborators. At that point, I write a first draft, which is the crucial phase. Changes from one draft to the next are major structural changes. I don't tamper, I always write complete drafts. *Toto* was written in seven drafts.

PH: *You must find yourself straining against the constraints.*

JVD: Not at all. They're a help. Despite its complexity, there is nothing innovative about the construction of *Toto*: the story and the style are too strange to withstand any kind of structural monkey business. In fact, the whole thing is like the *Palais du Facteur Cheval*, a crazy house built by a provincial French postman in the 1890s, which the surrealists loved because they thought it epitomized the 'automatic' principles of their art. Close up, it looks like a heap of mad, accumulated matter, but from a distance you can see the shape of a proper château beneath the lunacy.

The Rules of the Trade

JVD: At first I was very scornful of screenwriting 'rules', but once I started writing I found they were essential. Now I trust them, I feel confident enough to make deliberate mistakes and advertise those mistakes. Mistakes become stylistic devices when you are in a position to choose what mistakes you want to make.

PH: *I always try and think of films that don't comply with the rules of screenwriting.*

JVD: There aren't any. That is what is so astonishing. Frank Daniel is brilliant at analysing films. When he read my screenplay, he said, we're going to make *Amarcord*. What he meant by that is that we're going to make a film which seems completely crazy, but in fact is highly structured. *Amarcord* is constructed along strictly classical lines with three-act sub-plots, the main acts syncopated so the first act contains a scene from the second, the second act of story A comes before the third act of story C and so on. The story is built around a sequence of triple-act stories, a three-point rhythm contained within a superstructure which is the fête – the fête itself has three acts, of course. The lesson from *Amarcord* is that you can be as complicated as you like provided you obey the rules: it is when you don't obey the rules that a story feels clumsy and unnatural.

The odd thing about Frank Daniel is that he tends to concentrate on old movies, movies from the 1940s, because the construction of those films is easier to describe, but when he screens *Amarcord* he cries. 1940s films don't make him cry.

PH: *When you see a movie, are you aware of the construction?*

JVD: No.

PH: *You forget all the technical side?*

JVD: Yes. I watch the characters, I believe what they are going through. If it is a good film, I forget I am in a cinema, otherwise I'd be bored stiff!

PH: *Do you see more films now than when you were seventeen?*

JVD: Yes, because now I like films that are flawed. When I was seventeen I would have been bothered by the fact that a film didn't work and was badly made, or by a lopsided story, whereas now there's always something for me to learn from in the mistakes. I am more demanding in one respect now though: I demand of a film that it should say something important; I expect to come out of the cinema having had a life-changing experience or to have learnt something about life. If I don't get that I can still enjoy the movie, but it isn't the same thing. What really makes a film worthwhile is the feeling that it has introduced me to a new set of people and allowed me to share in a slice of their lives. I liked *Riff-Raff*, the Ken Loach movie. It was a life-changing experience.

PH: *Why? Did you like the way he developed his characters?*

JVD: I liked the truth of what he had to say. I liked the fact that what he is saying is crucially true and important.

Shooting is a Series of Headaches

JVD: It is in the writing and then again in the editing that a director is closest to narrative. Shooting is a series of headaches. You have to achieve a certain number of correct decisions within a fixed amount of time. Of course, I like working with actors and with technicians, but the best bit is in the dreaming. That is a quote from Pasolini. I get much more fun out of rehearsing the actors than directing them on set, because in rehearsal I can make mistakes, I can change my mind. I can when I'm writing too. A writer rereads what he has written the morning after. Same in the cutting room: you go back over what you've done once you are detached enough to know what might be wrong. In writing, editing, rehearsal you can change things. Not while you are shooting. There's always that moment when you know that a shot has got to be finished in the next twenty minutes or dropped altogether.

PH: *How many takes do you do?*

JVD: As many as I need.

PH: *Jacques Doillon, the French director, is famous for doing sixty-seven takes . . .*

JVD: I do somewhere between two and twelve. Usually the second take is the best. From then on, you're more likely to lose as much as you gain. And you lose the ability to tell whether a take is good or not. Doing lots of takes works for impulsive directors who know immediately whether a take is good or not. I am someone who needs to sit back and think.

From Writing to Shooting . . .

JVD: A writer's brain cannot anticipate every detail of performance, of an actor's physiognomy. If you could plug a lead into the writer's brain and transmit directly everything he imagines on to the screen, you'd get something much less powerful than what you get after the director has had to battle with actors, with lights and a set. Film needs the chaos of real life. You say *Toto the Hero* is very meticulous, but I actually think it is quite approximate. The emotions I am trying to describe are very precise in my mind and I hope in the audience's mind, which is what makes it a good, memorable film. But the actual sounds and images captured are approximations of life.

A film consists not in what is on the screen, but in what remains in the audience's mind when they leave the cinema. When the lights go up, at the end of a performance, the audience takes the heart of a film home. The imprecision and flaws stay behind in the empty picture palace. Of course, the audience is taking home precisely those ideas and images which inspired the writer and the director to make the film in the first place, often years before.

The germ of an idea for a film is something so imprecise it

cannot be described, a portion of chaos. And the whole process of writing is one of pinning things down, of working and reworking the scenes till they distil into a set of specific characters in specific places doing specific things at a specific time.

Reading a scene one has just written is always disappointment. 'Oh, that's all it was.' Then, as you rework it, as you go into it again and again, you discover more and more of the detail and so you catch a glimpse of what it was that inspired you in the first place. Eventually, if the scene is well-written, it will contain a replica of the original emotion which first made you want to write it. And that is what you are after when you start shooting.

And from Shooting to Editing . . .

JVD: I call shooting shopping. You know what the dish is, so you go out and find the ingredients. You want them to be as fresh as possible, you want a bit of variety. You know that if something is missing, you'll have to make do with something else. But the main thing is to get all the ingredients into that shopping bag and get the shopping bag into the kitchen – the cutting room.

PH: *The film feels story-boarded.*

JVD: I draw quite badly, but drawing is the best way I know of thinking things out. Even if no one was going to see my storyboard, I'd still have one. As it is, I hand it out to the crew, which saves time because it tells everyone exactly what is going to be in shot and what isn't – or what is *supposed* to be in shot because, in the end, I suppose everything always turns out unexpectedly. The real reason I use a storyboard is that it represents my mental images as closely as possible. For instance, it shows the surface relationships between characters, where people should stand, how the image is going to be ordered and that in itself is a part of the meaning of the shot – it is a first step. In a sketch I can work things out ahead of time, changing my angles, or switching one character from foreground to background; I can move everything, people, furniture, the shape of the space in a second, whereas on set it would involve taking a window out and so on – it would be impossible.

PH: *Do you sketch scenes out as you are writing them or only after the script is complete?*

JVD: When it is finished. But the images are there at the time of writing as clearly as if I were sitting in a cinema describing what I was seeing and hearing. That is what a script is: it is a formal device for recording what one wishes to see and wishes to hear. When I reread a script I know the images I imagined when I was writing it and I hear the sounds I imagined too.

PH: *Do you think you could write plays?*

JVD: I have written plays, long ago. But that isn't how I like to work in the theatre. My experience in the theatre is that we always improvised, there was never an author, or at least everyone was the author, a collective author, we would improvise endless scenes and then cut away all the bad stuff till we had got it right. The process is the same as scriptwriting, except that it is collective.

PH: *There are people who make films that way, by improvising.*

JVD: I've done that, turned up the morning of the shoot with two sentences of dialogue on an index card and then taken it from there. We did it in *Toto* in the scenes in the mental home. That was one of the bits I enjoyed most, probably because I had no idea what was going to happen and I knew I was going to ask the patients to do one thing and they would inevitably do something else which was much much better.

PH: *Those scenes feel as if they have been shot differently.*

JVD: They were. I mean, all I could do really was to roughly define a space for the patients to occupy and let them get on with it. Of course, I told them what I was after and they produced something related, but different. Every take came as a surprise. But it all had tremendous energy. They enjoyed themselves. And it is wonderfully gratifying to have something new in every take. Actors have an enormous amount of self-control which makes it hard for them to improvise in front of a camera. It works much better with people who don't govern everything they do, like children or lunatics. With them, improvisation can be brilliant because no one is in control, least of all me. You have to be on the same wavelength as your actors. With professional actors you must be professional, you must be technical and thoughtful. Some need a lot of technical guidance; some want to be left alone; some need their hand held every inch of the way. My job is to find the key, to get on the right wavelength. That's why I enjoyed working with Célestin, the lunatic brother in *Toto*, because it meant I had to become lunatic too. The continuity girl would say you've got 40 metres left, will that do? And I would say, I have no idea. I would give directions like, 'Then you sing a song and kiss him and . . .' off he would go and we had no idea what we were going to get. It was crazy.

PH: *Would it be fair to say that you have discovered a formula in the combination of meticulous construction with moments of complete improvisation ?*

JVD: I have no idea what I am going to do next and the only thing I do know is that I would like each film to be radically different. In *Toto* I managed to cram quite a few different styles into the one film, which was good because I need variety. One of my slogans is that I most admire films when you cannot tell who directed them. I admire that because it suggests to me the style chosen was a function of what the story required and not a limitation imposed on the story by the director's subjective concerns. Having said which, people have said about *Toto*, 'What a weird film, it's so complicated', but to me it isn't weird at all because that is how I think.

PH: *But surely if a film is to be at all personal, then the director's own style must be apparent?*

JVD: OK, but you can feel a strong director behind a film, without knowing who the director is, as soon as you have seen the first three shots. Signature shots. I'd love to make films in the style of Cassavetes, I'd love to have that freedom, just to work on the actors, to shoot actors . . . that would be amazing.

PH: *Just once, as an experiment?*

JVD: At least once. My shorts are all made in different styles and I'd like all my films to be in different genres. I've made lots of documentaries, improvised films, one musical, comedy, tragedy, completely experimental things, completely incomprehensible things, just trying out new things all the time.

PH: *Does everyone on set have a copy of the script?*

JVD: Yes. And a shooting script. And a storyboard. And everyone is allowed to see the rushes. But no one is allowed into the cutting room. The cutting room is the secret place where rhythm and precision and meaning are restored. Of course, your first impression on seeing the rushes is exactly the same as when you first sat down to write the script. You think, 'Oh, so that's all it was.' Then, gradually, as you get down to work in the cutting room, as you weed things out, shorten some bits, build up other bits, as you manufacture a structure, the thing you're after begins to emerge: the thing that originally made you want to make the film, which is what the audience will take away with them – a way of looking at the world. And giving people a new way of looking at the world is what film does.

PH: *How long did it take to edit* Toto?

JVD: Six months, I think, two thirds of which was sound editing. There were two sound editors, with two assistants just for sound. Sound is tremendously important; because it is invisible, it carries a disproportionate amount of the emotion in a film. Sound is nowhere near as meaningful as picture, but it is more tangible, more sensuous. Altering sound completely alters the atmosphere of a given scene. Sound governs the degree of tension. But the viewer has no idea of the effect of sound; he or she thinks that, because he sees the picture, he is somehow in control of his reaction to it, he can check whether a door is crooked or not and so on. He understands dialogue, he can recognize music – usually – and he hears sound that is transmitting concrete information. But viewers don't 'hear' abstract sound. Perhaps, if he or she concentrates very hard, a viewer may recognize up to three distinct simultaneous sounds out of a total of twenty or thirty on a given shot. And those other sounds really matter. Imagine having an argument with someone in a room, and your voices get louder and louder and louder until suddenly someone switches the air conditioning off and only then do you realize what was irritating you so much. I have been working with the same sound engineer, Dominique Warnier, since I started making films and we have developed a common language, we both know we are after the same thing.

PH: *There is one important difference between picture and sound and that is that the viewer chooses where to look on a big screen, whereas he cannot consciously choose which sounds to listen to.*

JVD: Absolutely. And you can use sound to shift the viewer's attention from the foreground to the background or vice versa. Sound is more than what is going on outside the frame, it is also like music, providing you aren't restricted to a realistic handling of sound. In fact, proper film sound is much more complex than music because there is no tempo, no notes. The brain uses beat to process music whereas sound is too chaotic for the brain to recognize; sound is quite crazy. The emotional charge of sound comes from the fact that the brain cannot process it. In *Toto*, the first fire scene in which the two babies are swapped wouldn't have worked at all without intense sound treatment. The number of different types of sound on the tape at that point is incredible. There are about thirty different sounds involved, and they all sound like a single sound.

PH: *What sounds are they?*

JVD: Sounds manufactured by the sound engineer, or sounds he already possessed, in his sound library – as I said, we have been working together for ten years – which we then manipulated, slowed down or reversed. For instance, in the fire in the maternity ward: a blacksmith's hammer, slowed down; screaming mothers and reversed screaming mothers, who sound like ululating wolves; slow motion steps; slow motion breaking glass, which sounds like bells, and ordinary breaking glass; there's a continuous bass sound of slow motion flames, a normal sound of guttering flames and a high-pitched flicker sound as well. The aim is to have sound from the bottom to the top of the register, and to place reversed or slowed-down sounds beside real-time sounds. There is a sound of babies crying, the sound of a fire alarm, of a fire engine, of wind whistling and so on. I can't remember half of them. But each sound creates its own particular atmosphere and together they denote confusion, panic, emotional upheaval.

A Story Emerges: Pacing

JVD: When you get into the cutting room some scenes need to be dropped because they slow the film down. Or sometimes the scene is fine, but the beginning and the end are too laborious. I know that as a writer I take too long to bring a scene to a climax and too long to finish it once it has achieved its purpose. You should go straight to the heart of a scene, cut straight to the action. Even then, the chances are it will still be too long.

There's another thing which you can only really get right in the cutting room and that is the business of exposition: when should a piece of information come? Even though you may think you've decided all that at script stage, the script conveys so much less information than the finished film that some elements of exposition are going to have to be changed. If a script had to describe everything people were going to see and hear, it would be unreadable, and thousands of pages long; there would be no rhythm to it. The way a script reads tells you the intended pace of a film. I like a page to represent about fifty seconds of film time, that's the pace I like.

PH: *Is that a fixed rule or is it just an average?*

JVD: It is a fixed rule, it's quite a lot of work. Usually people reckon on about a minute per page.

PH: *What about description? Do you give detailed descriptions of sets, sound, music and so on?*

JVD: No, most of the time I don't include descriptions of locations in the script or, if I do write them, I put them to one side and give them to the designer as notes – unless they are essential to understanding the script. For instance, if there's a shot that lasts several minutes, I am almost bound to describe the set because I want the time it takes to read the description to relate to the time the shot will last. If, on the other hand, a location is not described in the script, even though it will be shown on film, that simply means that things are moving fast at that particular juncture.

A director's style is the sum of his mistakes; the mistakes he makes regularly. They are an expression of what he is afraid of, which is a function of style too. I believe that directors who are afraid of people are more likely to use wide shots and be reluctant to have an actor face the camera directly. Some people are terrified of cutting and try to avoid doing so; they shoot in extended *plan-séquences* in an attempt to get most of the editing over during shooting.

My own phobia is pace. If I have to shoot a scene, eight weeks after shooting a related scene, I cannot spontaneously recall the rhythm we had found. Pacing is critical. You need to remember changes of rhythm, you need to know when narrative should speed up or slow down. I find myself varying the angles as much as possible so that I can delay having to deal with pacing until I get into the cutting room. The trouble with this is that sometimes multiple camera angles are wrong, sometimes you just want the story to pause for a bit and stay where it is. Then, of course, you need to use fewer, longer shots which means setting the pace on set, within the real time of the shot.

In *Toto* there is one such moment: when the two children are in bed together, bang in the middle of the film. That shot has to be held as long as possible because there is no reason to cut it, so I told the kids to hold their breath and take as much time as they possibly dared. But that's an exception. Usually I want to construct the rhythm of a scene at the editing table, because pace dictates the audience's perception of a story, it makes the emotion.

Another thing I am terrified of: being boring. That fear is another component of my style. It means I have to go very fast. I want to keep the audience on its toes, not waiting around while I harp on about something they already know.

Suppose a character has to stand up and leave. The action cannot take place in real time. It has to take place in the time it takes to realize what he is going to do. The film has to be one step ahead of the spectator's imagination, so that it drives his brain. The purpose is not to reproduce reality, but to plunge people into a narrative. The purpose is to manipulate the audience.

The faster a film is, the more direct it becomes. If a film is slow, it feels intellectual. *Toto*, shot more slowly, would have been an 'intellectual' film, for art houses only, because the slower a film is, the more time it gives the audience to watch and think and interpret; whereas by going very fast, you force the brain to let go, analysis goes out the window, it's left behind, it can't keep up – and all that's left is sensual emotion and feeling. You address people's senses and affections. If anyone's going to think about the structure of a film, the director is, not the audience. The director should devise the structure so cunningly that by the time it reaches the screen, it is invisible. If an audience has to focus on structure, it won't recognize its emotions.

PH: *One of the effects of your way of writing is that it makes for a very dense film, packed with observation, so that there is something for everyone in it. I am sure that is part of the reason for its success.*

JVD: The film is definitely a broad church, definitely chaotic and, in that respect, it is very realistic. Life is chaotic.

This introduction and interview first appeared in a different form in Projections 2, Faber and Faber, London, 1993.

Toto the Hero was first shown at the 1991 Cannes Film Festival where it won the Camera D'Or for the Best First Film. The cast and crew includes:

OLD THOMAS	Michael Bouquet
ADULT THOMAS	Jo De Backer
YOUNG THOMAS	Thomas Godet
OLD EVELYNE	Gisela Uhlen
ADULT EVELYNE	Mireille Perrier
ALICE	Sandrine Blancke
OLD ALFRED	Peter Bohlke
ADULT ALFRED	Didier Ferney
YOUNG ALFRED	Hugo Harold Harrison
THOMAS'S MOTHER	Fabienne Loriaux
THOMAS'S FATHER	Klaus Schindler
ADULT CELESTIN	Pascal Duquenne
YOUNG CELESTIN	Karim Moussati
MONSIEUR KANT	Didier de Neck
MADAM KANT	Christine Smeysters
THE INSPECTOR	Roland de Pauw
Director of Photography	Walther Van den Ende
Art Director	Hubert Pouille
Set Design	Frederic Huwaert
Editor	Susana Rossberg
Sound Editor	Chantal Hymans
Original Score	Pierre Van Dormael
Co-Producers	Philippe Dussart
	Luciano Gloor
Executive Producers	Pierre Drouot
	Dany Geys
Screenplay	Jaco Van Dormael
Director	Jaco Van Dormael

An Ibis Film, Les Productions Philippe Dussart, Metropolis Film production.

INT. 'LES ROSES' VILLA. NIGHT

A few drops of rain on a window. Sound of breaking glass. A window-pane shatters and falls in a star pattern around a small hole: a bullet hole. Fragments of glass sparkle in the air before bouncing off the ground. A few drops of rain splatter on the parquet floor. A draught billows through the curtain. The curtain tautens and rips.

A hand lies on the floor, inanimate. A small cellophane sweet-wrapper falls out of the hand. It rolls on the ground, driven by the wind. A tuft of white hair ruffled by the draught. Police sirens in the distance.

> OLD THOMAS
> (*voice-over*)

I'll kill you, Alfred.

INT. 'LES ROSES' VILLA. NIGHT

Photographic flashes. A motionless, old man's corpse stretched on the ground. His face lies in the water of a small fountain dug into the ground. The torn curtain is wrapped around his neck. A policeman marks the outline of the body on the ground using a strip of adhesive tape. In his hand, the old man is clutching an artificial rose.

About ten policemen are at work in a large living-room. The furniture is covered in dust-sheets, as if the house had been left empty.

A small black fingerprint brush spreads a dirty layer of black dust on the door-knobs. The space between the wall and the dead man's shoe is measured. Sweets scattered on the ground. A pair of tweezers delicately lifts one. A puzzled inspector studies it. He slips it into a small plastic bag.

> OLD THOMAS
> (*voice-over; quavering*)

Those cops! What can they possibly make of it? That you were strangled in a curtain, drowned and shot in the back? Ha ha!. . . No one will ever think of accusing me.

The corpse is raised. Its head cannot be seen as it comes out of the water. Sound of dripping water.

INT. ROOM IN A RETIREMENT HOME. NIGHT

Sound of dripping water. Old Thomas holds his head in his hands as he bends over a washbasin. Water flows through his fingers. He stands straight. Moving around the back of his neck, we discover his face in the glass. He examines himself. Thomas is about seventy. He rubs the wrinkles in his cheek.

> OLD THOMAS
> (*voice-over*)
> No one will recognize me after all these years. Not even you.

He passes a white flannel over his face.

INT. 'LES ROSES' VILLA. NIGHT

Two hands cover the old man's corpse in a white sheet. He is slipped into a plastic body-bag. A hand closes the zip. . .

INT. ROOM IN A RETIREMENT HOME. NIGHT

Thomas's hand buttons his pyjamas. He gets into bed and switches the light out. His eyes remain open.

> OLD THOMAS
> (*voice-over*)
> It won't be a murder. It'll only be me reclaiming what's mine: the life you stole the day I was born. . .
> (*In shot*)
> My life!

INT. MATERNITY WARD CORRIDOR. NIGHT

1957. A smoky corridor. In slow motion, mothers in towelling dressing-gowns run around in panic. Screams. Flames lick at the windows. Glass shatters. A slipper is trodden underfoot.

INT. INFANTS' WARD. NIGHT

In the distance, panic-stricken cries. In the infants' ward, two babies cry in neighbouring cots. They both have brown hair with a bit of a natural quiff.

INT. MATERNITY WARD CORRIDOR. NIGHT

Commotion. Through the door, which is ajar, the television in the nurses' room is on: black-and-white television image. . .

EXT. TV IMAGE. THOMAS'S STREET. NIGHT

Suspense music. Toto the secret agent, wearing a raincoat and soft hat, shoots from behind a car. A warehouse explodes. Flames burst out. . .

INT. INFANTS' WARD. NIGHT

Terrified mothers burst into the nursery and try to recognize their babies among the rows of cots. They lift them up and stare into their faces. . . Panic-stricken nurses run all over the place.

Baby Thomas yells in his cot. A woman (Mrs Kant) runs up. Her face is not visible. She grabs Thomas, hesitates, leans into the neighbouring cot, puts Thomas back and takes the other baby. Thomas watches them run off. Another woman (Thomas's mother) appears, sees the empty cot, shrieks, sees Thomas, hesitates, takes him and runs off with him. The two cots remain side by side, empty. Their pillows catch fire. Smoke.

> OLD THOMAS
> (*voice-over*)
> The Good Lord must have been picking his nose. One moment's inattention and Bob's your uncle. You've lived my life. Thief!

INT. ROOM IN A RETIREMENT HOME. NIGHT

Old Thomas's face on his pillow as he smokes a cigarette. He stubs it out.

Old Thomas sits up in bed. It is still dark outside. He switches on a bedside light. The room is small and square, with anonymous-looking furniture. There are books piled on the bedside table.

Bare-chested, he stands at his washbasin and washes. Every gesture takes a considerable amount of time.

He puts his socks on. One of them has a hole in it.

INT. ROOM IN A RETIREMENT HOME. DAY

Someone knocks at the door. Thomas is seated at a small Formica table. He appears to be waiting patiently. A Nurse enters and puts a breakfast tray in front of him. Thomas ignores her. He checks the amount of jam. The nurse takes his fingers and examines them. There is a yellow stain between his index and third fingers.

> NURSE
> Have you been smoking again?

Thomas furiously removes his hand.

> I warned you! No day out for you this week!

The Nurse takes two tablets from a bottle and puts them on the tray.

INT. ROOM IN A RETIREMENT HOME. DAY

Quick flash: Thomas grabs the bottle from the nurse, pours all the tablets out into the palm of his hand and stuffs them into the nurse's mouth as she screams.

INT. ROOM IN A RETIREMENT HOME. DAY

Back to normal. Thomas takes the two tablets off the tray and swallows them. The nurse leaves. Thomas listens to her steps retreating.

INT. 'LES ROSES' VILLA. DAY

A muffled buzzing. The corpse on the ground.

> OLD THOMAS
> (*voice-over*)
> It's so easy. So perfect. All I need to do is ring the doorbell. . .

INT. KANT HOME. DAY

Quick flashes: a finger on the doorbell, the door opens, a stranger's aged face. Thomas examines the old man, points a revolver through the doorframe . . .

> OLD THOMAS
> (*voice-over*)

You open the door and bang!

INT. ROOM IN A RETIREMENT HOME. DAY

Thomas smokes, pensively.

> OLD THOMAS
> (*murmuring; in shot*)

Bang!

> (*voice-over*)

You won't even know it's me. You won't recognize me. You won't know why I've shot you. But I know. I've forgotten nothing, Alfred. Nothing.

INT.EXT. VARIOUS. DAY/NIGHT

Quick flashes: a fist in child Thomas's belly. Another boy, Alfred, beats him up. Alfred, adult now, drunk in a bar, laughing at someone. A knife dropped in a river. Thomas's mother's face covered in blood. A warehouse fire. Babies swapped.

INT. RETIREMENT HOME REFECTORY. DAY

Old Thomas eating, surrounded by other old men. It is hot. A fan spins on the ceiling.

> OLD THOMAS
> (*voice-over*)

There's nothing but old men here. I hate old men. They spend their time at the cemetery and they'll certainly end up there for good.

INT. ROOM IN A RETIREMENT HOME. NIGHT

Standing bare-chested at his washbasin, old Thomas washes. A flannel glove moves slowly up his arm towards the shoulder.

INT. THOMAS'S APARTMENT. DAY

Flash: young woman's (Evelyne's) hand caresses adult Thomas's shoulder.

133

INT. ROOM IN A RETIREMENT HOME. NIGHT

Old Thomas sits on his bed. He switches the light off. He undresses. He lays his head on his pillow.

INT. ALICE'S ROOM. NIGHT

Alice's face bends over child Thomas as he lies in bed. She kisses him.

INT. ROOM IN A RETIREMENT HOME. NIGHT

Old Thomas turns in bed. He watches:

INT. THOMAS'S APARTMENT. DAY

. . . Evelyne watching him. Adult Thomas makes love to Evelyne. They kiss and roll over on the bed.

INT. ROOM IN A RETIREMENT HOME. NIGHT

Old Thomas holds back his tears.

> OLD THOMAS
> (*voice-over*)

You stole my life. You stole my love. I lived nothing. Nothing happened.

His eyes are moist. He looks out of the window. . .

. . . my story's the story of a guy nothing ever happens to.

> OLD THOMAS
> (*in shot*)

Nothing.

EXT. STARS. NIGHT

Through the window: a starry sky.

Dissolve to: a constellation . . . galaxies spinning in time with the music.

A Title: TOTO THE HERO

The title disappears. Nothing but stars. Then a grey pebble of no particular shape moving towards us, grazing past us.

> YOUNG THOMAS
> (*voice-over*)

Once upon a time there was a little bit of nothing in particular that came from nowhere at all . . .

EXT. STUDIO — SEA. NIGHT

Night. Waves ruffling water. Something falls in with a 'plop' . . .

> YOUNG THOMAS
> (*voice-over*)

Then it fell in: plop!

A large model sailing-ship appears, propelled by a giant hand. . .

A big white boat found him and brought him to his parents. That's what his mother used to tell him.

Swirling fog fills the screen.

INT. INFANTS' WARD. NIGHT

The smoke parts. Two cots in flames.

INT. BATHROOM. DAY

Baby Thomas (aged one) pulls his head out of the water, wide-eyed with surprise.

His father and mother's head, against the ceiling.

> YOUNG THOMAS
> (*voice-over*)

So then they introduced him to his daddy and his mummy. They told him his name was Thomas Van Hasebroeck, that it was 1957 and that there was nothing he could do about it.

INT. LIVING-ROOM. DAY

A baby's hand (aged one) presses down on a piano key. The Mother's mouth forms the words of a song, 'Hey ho the firemen'.

(*voice-over*)

His mother called him the little baby. The little baby knew
how to sing. (*Mumbling*) Hey-ho the firemen, the house is
burning down. . . it wasn't me that burned it down, it was a
little man. . .

The baby's hands grasp the mother's hand as she spins.

And then his mother would dance!

The mother's hand taking wet sheets off a child's bed.

When you do a pee, it's warm and then it goes cold. There's a
funny smell . . .

*Two enormous, smiling heads lean over us: the Father is right way up,
the Mother is upside down.*

Mummy smells nicer than Daddy. Daddy has hair under his
nose and a hat on his head.

The baby's hand tugs at the cat's tail. It mews.

When you pull the cat's tail, he yells.

The baby hits its mother with a spoon.

When you hit Mummy, she yells.

Suddenly, a model plane drops on to the floor. A child's shoe treads on it.

The plane doesn't yell. You can throw it and tread on it.

*The Father kisses the Mother as she bites into a slice of bread. A little
girl wearing a blue dress (Alice, aged four), is seated at the breakfast
table, her face bent over a bowl of milk.*

CHILD THOMAS
(*voice-over*)

In the mornings, Daddy kisses Mummy and Mummy kisses
her little boy, meaning me!

Thomas (aged one) looks in the mirror. Laughingly, he hits at his reflection.

In the mornings, Daddy goes behind the door. If you go and

peek behind it, he's gone: he's at work.

Seen from behind, Thomas (aged three) runs towards the door and opens it. There's no one there.

INT. LIVING-ROOM. NIGHT

The Father comes in with a smile. Alice (aged six), wearing a blue dress, runs and hangs on to his neck.

> YOUNG THOMAS
> (*voice-over*)
> In the evenings, Daddy opens the door. He's back. He was behind the door, but he was invisible because he was behind it.

INT. PARENTS' ROOM. DAY

> YOUNG THOMAS
> (*voice-over*)
> Daddy's funny. He hides and then he can't be seen any more.

Thomas and Alice (aged three and six, seen from behind, or aged eight and eleven but dressed as before) run through their parents' room, shouting . . . Alice opens the wardrobe: the Father's shoes peep out from beneath the clothes . . . the Father parts the clothes and laughs. He hugs Thomas and Alice and gives them sweets.

INT. THOMAS'S ROOM. NIGHT

Thomas (aged eight) is in bed with his eyes open. The room is dark.

> YOUNG THOMAS
> (*voice-over*)
> At night, it's dark. You can't see anything at all.

EXT. STREET. DAY

A dead cat by the road.

> YOUNG THOMAS
> (*voice-over*)
> Cats don't see anything at all either when they're dead. They lie nice and still.

INT. 'LES ROSES' VILLA. NIGHT

The old man's corpse on the ground. Red sweets scattered all around.

INT. LIVING-ROOM. DAY

The Father shows Thomas a red sweet, just like the sweets seen around the corpse. He takes the sweet in his other hand and mouths the word 'abracadabra'.

> YOUNG THOMAS
> (*voice-over*)
>
> Abracadabra.

The Father opens his hand: the sweet has vanished!

> The sweet's at work!

EXT. YOUNG THOMAS'S STREET. DAY

Thomas comes out of his house holding his Daddy's hand. On the opposite pavement, Alfred (aged eight) holding Mr Kant's hand. Alfred has a duck's tail in his dark hair, just like Thomas's. The two children stare at each other. The adults politely raise their hats.

> YOUNG THOMAS
> (*voice-over*)
>
> The neighbour's Daddy is called Daddy too. Daddies are gentlemen. But his Daddy is not the same as mine.

INT. LIVING-ROOM. DAY

The Father is at the piano. He gives a big smile and sings in the style of Charles Trenet:

> FATHER
> (*singing*)
>
> *La pendule fait tic-tac, tic-tic. Les oiseaux du lac plic-plac, plic-plic.*[1]

The children listen, sitting next to each other on the couch. Thomas

---

1 The clock goes tick-tock, tick-tick. The birds on the lake go plick-plack, plick-plick.

(aged eight), Alice (aged eleven) and Célestin (aged five), a child with Down's syndrome, sitting on the mother's knees. Thomas and Alice turn to one another. Discreetly, they take each other's hands. They are content.

EXT. YOUNG THOMAS'S STREET. DAY

> **FATHER**
> *Glou-glou-glou font les dindons . . .*[1]

Over the music, Thomas's house, with its little garden, bathed in sunshine. A row of multicoloured tulips swings in time to the music . . .

> **SONG**
> *Et la jolie cloche ding-dang-dong . . .*[2]

A (mechanical) butterfly lands on a flower.

A bright yellow Ford passes slowly by the house. A woman smiles and waves. Outside his house, Thomas's Father washes his car with a hose.

INT. LIVING-ROOM. DAY

> **SONG**
> But boom!

A banger explodes on the table and sends up a cloud of confetti. There is a birthday cake in front of Thomas. He blows the candles out. Alice and Célestin clap. The mother films the scene with a small 8mm camera. Thomas unwraps his present: a red model car.

> **SONG**
> *Lorsque not' coeur fait boum!*[3]

The Father is at the piano. Alice plays the trumpet.

> **SONG**
> *Tout avec lui dit boum*
> *Et c'est l'amour qui s'éveille . . .*[4]

1 Glug-glug-glug go the turkeys . . .
2 And the lovely bell rings ding-a-ling-ling . . .
3 When our heart goes boom!
4 Everything else goes boom
  And love starts a-stirring . . .

Thomas and Alice stare into each other's eyes and smile. The music ends.

INT./EXT. THOMAS'S ROOM. DAY

Thomas is at the window, holding his red model car. He is watching . . .

EXT. ALFRED'S GARDEN (POV: WINDOW) DAY

In the garden of the house across the road, at a garden table, Alfred too blows out the candles on a birthday cake. His parents, Mr and Mrs Kant, laugh and clap.

> YOUNG THOMAS
> (*voice-over*)
> The neighbour's name is Alfred. His birthday's the same day as mine.

Alfred unwraps his present: a red pedal car.

INT. LIVING-ROOM. NIGHT

An 8mm image on a white wall. Thomas watches amazed from the shadows.

INT. 8MM IMAGES, LIVING-ROOM. DAY

Thomas blows out the candles on his cake. Laughingly, he holds his red model car out to the camera. The focus slips. Older images: the mother carrying a baby, a baby crawling.

EXT. 8MM IMAGES, AIRPORT. DAY

The Father loads crates into a private plane. The plane has the name of a cargo company written on the side. The Father waves for the camera. The plane takes off. Flash. The Father disembarks from the plane and poses with pride. He laughs. He drags the Mother in front of the camera and kisses her.

> YOUNG THOMAS
> (*voice-over*)
> Daddy drives planes. One day he fell into Mummy's garden and stayed.

EXT. THOMAS'S STREET. DAY

Naïve style: the Father wearing an airman's outfit dropping by parachute in front of the house. The Mother is by the door. He takes her into his arms with tenderness. The parachute obscures them. It is white.

INT. PARENTS' ROOM. DAY

The Mother lies in bed under a white sheet. She is smoking a cigarette. The Father kisses her hand.

> YOUNG THOMAS
> (*voice-over*)
> Then he licked her hand. Mummy smoked a cigarette and Alice was born.

INT. BATHROOM. DAY

Alice and Thomas, face to face and naked in the bath. They look each

other up and down, intrigued. Total silence. Sound of water lapping.
Their feet touch. They laugh. Thomas takes Alice's hand and gives it
great licks. Alice laughs.

EXT. THOMAS'S STREET. DAY

Passers-by outside the house watching Célestin standing on a first-floor
window-ledge. His arms are spread, as though he is about to fly off. The
Mother appears behind him and just manages to catch him.

INT. KITCHEN. DAY

> YOUNG THOMAS
> (*voice-over*)

Célestin was born in a washing-machine. That's why he's
funny.

Washing spinning in a washing-machine drum.

INT. LIVING-ROOM. DAY

Célestin playing an educational game: he tries to push a cube into a
round hole. This does not work. His expression is gentle.

INT. THOMAS'S ROOM. NIGHT

Thomas is in bed, with his eyes open.

> YOUNG THOMAS
> (*voice-over*)

I was born in a fire. Mummy said it wasn't true, but I
remember.

INT. INFANTS' WARD. NIGHT

Baby Thomas yells in his cot. Swirling smoke. In slow motion, Mrs
Kant lifts Thomas and stares at him. She examines the baby in the next
cot, hesitates and puts Thomas down. Thomas yells. Mrs Kant runs off
carrying baby Alfred. Thomas's Mother appears and sees Alfred's empty
cot. She shrieks, sees Thomas, hesitates . . .

INT./EXT. THOMAS'S ROOM. DAY

From the window, Thomas looks over at the house across the road.

EXT. ALFRED'S GARDEN (POV: WINDOW) DAY

The house across the road is impressive. It sits in the middle of a well-maintained lawn. Mrs Kant stands at the door, holding Alfred by the hand. At the bottom of the garden, there is a hangar with the word 'Kant' written on it. A truck fills up at a petrol pump. In the background, a swimming-pool is visible. A beautiful Jaguar car with polished chrome fittings comes into the drive. An elegantly dressed man gets out: this is Mr Kant. Alfred runs up to him and hangs on his neck.

EXT. ALFRED'S GARDEN. DAY

Alfred plays on the lawn in his red pedal car. Thomas appears the other side of the fence. He watches Alfred. They have the same haircut, but Alfred looks tougher than Thomas.

> THOMAS
> Hey! Alfred! I want to tell you something!

Alfred looks up at Thomas. He approaches. Thomas takes a step back, out of reach. He says nothing.

> ALFRED
> Well, Van Chickensoup? What have you got to say?

> THOMAS
> Listen. Your parents aren't your parents, because they're mine. We were swapped when we were little.

Alfred stares at Thomas. Thomas examines the pedal car.

> Your parents are my parents and mine are yours. No one noticed because it was during the fire. It's true though. Your house and your car and the swimming-pool are mine too.

Alfred glares at Thomas. He goes pale. His fists tighten. Suddenly, Thomas appears to fold in half. Alfred's fist has shot out. Thomas falls on the ground.

ALFRED

If you tell anyone, you're dead, I swear. Do you hear? I'll kill
you.

Thomas is doubled up and breathless.

INT. 'LES ROSES' VILLA. NIGHT

OLD THOMAS
(*voice-over*)
Kill me then! What are you waiting for?

*The old man's corpse in its plastic body-bag . . . The corpse is laid on a
stretcher and picked up by ambulancemen, who carry it past Mr Kant's
portrait. In the picture, he poses by a hangar marked 'Kant'.*

EXT. TV IMAGE. DAY

*High-definition television image with subtitles in several languages and
inserts including, in a medallion, a rough montage of trembling images
showing ultra-modern factories marked 'Kant'. A few angry faces in a
crowd.*

VOICE-OVER COMMENTARY
Yesterday afternoon, the Kant Investment Company
bankruptcy angered hundreds of small shareholders, who feel
cheated. Alfred Kant, who has been in charge of the company
for the last forty years, since taking over from his father, has
had to flee, after an assassination attempt . . .

Bullet holes in a wall, marked out in chalk.

INT. RETIREMENT HOME REFECTORY. DAY

*These images are shown on a television which hangs from the ceiling.
Ten old men suffering from heat exhaustion sit clustered around a fan,
on uncomfortable chairs provided by the retirement home, watching
television. Only old Thomas displays any interest. He is unshaven,
dressed in a jacket over his pyjamas. He glares at the TV through his
glasses.*

EXT. TV IMAGE. DAY

High-definition television image of an old man trying to climb into a Jaguar and hide behind a newspaper at the same time. He is protected by security guards. The crowd insults him, tries to grab hold of him. A lady hits him with her handbag. The picture is obscured by a hand.

VOICE-OVER COMMENTARY
According to our latest information, Alfred Kant has taken refuge in a secret hiding place . . .

INT. RETIREMENT HOME CORRIDOR AND PORTER'S LODGE. NIGHT

Old Thomas watches the doorkeeper sip his cup of coffee as he watches a portable television set. The doorkeeper opens a drawer for more sugar. There's a gun and a box in the drawer. The phone rings. The doorkeeper does not reply. Thomas stares at the revolver.

INT. LIVING-ROOM. NIGHT

The doorbell rings insistently. A light goes on. The Mother comes to the door in her towelling dressing-gown. It's raining. Mr Kant is outside in a soaking-wet raincoat.

INT. THOMAS'S ROOM. NIGHT

Young Thomas is in bed. Sound of rain outside. He opens his eyes. Voices downstairs. The door of the room opens. A ray of light falls on Thomas. His Father sits on the edge of the bed and strokes his head without a word. He is wearing his coat. He says nothing. He smiles, worried. He continues to stroke Thomas's head in silence. As if by magic, he produces a sweet in the palm of his hand and gives it to Thomas. Then the Father takes his wristwatch off and gives it to Thomas.

FATHER
Keep it for me till I get home.

Thomas's Father kisses him. Thomas examines the watch. When he looks up, his Father has gone. Thomas gets out of bed and goes to the door, which remains ajar.

146

INT. CORRIDOR AND LIVING-ROOM (POV: THOMAS). NIGHT

Thomas goes towards the stairs and looks down through the banisters.
He can glimpse a canvas bag on the sitting-room floor, then two legs
moving towards the door. He sees his Mother from behind, half-
concealed, clutching a handkerchief in her fingers. She hugs the Father.
Mr Kant joins them.

> MR KANT
> (*softly*)

Let's go.

The Father picks up his bag.

> MOTHER
> (*softly*)

Look after yourself.

The Father kisses his wife. Then he leaves. Sound of the door closing.
Thomas runs back to his room.

INT. THOMAS'S ROOM. NIGHT

Thomas runs to his window.

EXT. THOMAS'S STREET (POV: WINDOW). NIGHT

Outside, it's pouring with rain. Two figures in a Jaguar: the Father
and Mr Kant. The car drives off. The street remains silent and deserted.

INT. THOMAS'S ROOM. NIGHT

The room is still in darkness. There is a lightning storm outside. Thomas
lies awake with his eyes wide open. He fidgets with a toy plane, flying it
back and forth over his head.

The hum of a plane drawing closer. The tooth-glass above the
washbasin starts to tinkle. A chandelier vibrates. The hum draws yet
closer. The chandelier imperceptibly sways. Thomas stares up at it. A
shelf above his bed vibrates too. Toy soldiers tremble and shift towards
the edge of the shelf. A flash of lightning illuminates the room. The
soldiers reach the edge and topple one after another into the void.
Thomas watches them fall. The sound of the plane disappears.

EXT. THOMAS'S STREET. DAY

The rain has stopped. The Jaguar is parked outside the house, behind a police car. Thomas is at his window.

INT. LIVING-ROOM. DAY

Wearing her towelling dressing-gown, the Mother sits in an armchair and cries. Mr Kant stands beside her. Two policemen are with him. They say nothing. Alice stares at Mr Kant.

Thomas comes downstairs in his pyjamas. No one takes any notice of him. He is clutching his toy plane.

Mr Kant seems put out. The Mother sobs.

> POLICEMAN
> Every possible kind of search is being conducted. There's nothing for it but to wait.

The Mother carries on sobbing.

> MR KANT
> I held your husband in high regard. If I had known, I would not have . . .

He falls silent. Thomas comes up to him. Mr Kant looks down at him with something like embarrassment. Thomas stares at his Mother in tears. Mr Kant kneels beside Thomas and points to the plane in his hands.

> It's a nice one . . . Is it yours?

Thomas does not reply.

> Can I have a look?

He holds out his hand. Thomas steps back and suddenly thumps Mr Kant on the head with his plane. This makes a thud. Mr Kant puts a hand to his forehead and falls backwards. He stands up again somewhat uncertainly. There is a spot of blood at his temple.

> MOTHER
> Thomas!

Thomas rushes back upstairs.

148

INT. PARENTS' ROOM. DAY

Thomas pushes the bedroom door open. The curtains are drawn. The bed is unmade. Suddenly the door of the wardrobe creaks . . . The door of the wardrobe in which the Father used to hide for hide-and-seek comes ajar. Through the crack, we watch Thomas approach. He opens the door: the father's shoes stick out from under the clothes that are hanging up there. Thomas yanks the clothes apart . . . The father's shoes are empty.

INT. LIVING-ROOM. DAY

Thomas is glued to a black-and-white television set.

EXT. TV IMAGE, THOMAS'S STREET. NIGHT

On the screen, a vintage French car is parked. Toto the secret agent sits behind the wheel. He strikes a match and takes a drag on his cigarette. The flame lights up his face.

INT. THOMAS'S ROOM. NIGHT

In the darkness, Thomas lies in bed with his eyes open.

YOUNG THOMAS
(*voice-over*)
When I'm grown up, I'll be a secret agent. Everyone'll say,
'Look!, there's Toto, the king of counter-espionage! His
daddy and his mummy are proud of him.'

EXT. THOMAS'S STREET. NIGHT

His face illuminated by the match, Toto the secret agent watches a
curtain part in one of the windows of Thomas's house. Thomas's Father
and Mother, older now, watch Toto. They are moved. They wave to
him.

Suddenly a Jaguar screeches to a halt. Four gangsters, including Mr
Kant, enter Thomas's house brandishing guns. Toto gets out of his car.
A burst of machine-gun fire throws him to the ground. The Mother
screams from the door. Toto raises his head and sees the four gangsters
drag his Father out of the house. They force him into their car. Toto
runs towards them. The car drives off. Toto shoots after them. The car
vanishes round a corner. Toto jumps into his car and races off after
them.

YOUNG THOMAS
(*voice-over*)
When I'm older, I'll rescue my daddy from the bad guys
who've captured him. And people will say, 'Look, there's
young Thomas, he's a secret agent now.'

INT. ROOM IN A RETIREMENT HOME. NIGHT

Old Thomas lies in bed, chuckling to himself in the dark.

OLD THOMAS
Secret agent! Ha ha ha!

He gets out of bed with difficulty. His back hurts. He goes to the basin
and pisses in it.

Ha ha ha! Secret agent!

INT. GOVERNMENT OFFICE CORRIDOR. DAY

The door to the toilets. Telephones ring. Sound of flushing. A civil servant appears. Another civil servant carrying a file questions him.

CIVIL SERVANT I

You haven't seen Thomas, have you?

CIVIL SERVANT 2

Isn't he in his office?

He carries on putting his head round a succession of doors. He encounters a group arguing by a coffee machine in the corridor. They can be heard in the distance.

DEPARTMENT HEAD

. . . it's staying here until the director says it can move.

CIVIL SERVANT 3

But what about all the people in room 310, what will they do? They've got to go right round the building for a cup of coffee.

CIVIL SERVANT 4

. . . *and* we're penalized when it comes to parking places.

INT. THOMAS'S OFFICE. DAY

A small, square room. It is impersonal: metal desk, chair, shelving. A man of about thirty, seated at a desk. He is seen from behind. On the desk, a small, framed photograph of Alice as a child, holding a trumpet.

YOUNG THOMAS
(*voice-over*)

And people will say, 'Look, there's young Thomas, he's a secret agent now.'

We move round and discover the man's face. This is adult Thomas. He looks like Toto the secret agent, except he's a little plumper. He wears spectacles and a tie. He has just sharpened a pencil and laid it tidily beside a row of other sharpened pencils. He stands and goes to a fish bowl containing a single goldfish . . .

And I'll marry a princess.

He pours a little food into the fish bowl.

THOMAS

Easy now, princess.

The civil servant who was looking for him opens the door and leaves a file on the desk.

CIVIL SERVANT I
Hi, Thomas.

He exits and leaves the door open. The phone rings. Thomas answers.

THOMAS
Hello? . . . Yes, speaking . . .

Silence. Thomas's expression turns a shade more serious.

Yes, I'm her son . . .? What? . . .

He listens. He turns his back to us . . . People pass by in the corridor, laughing. Thomas continues to listen . . . Silence . . . Thomas is motionless, lost in this office, with a receiver glued to his ear. Slowly, very slowly, he hangs up. He does not move. Through the window, all you can see is a wall. He stares at the wall.

INT. GOVERNMENT OFFICE CORRIDOR. DAY

Thomas comes out of his office. He is upset. He has put a raincoat on. He is carrying his briefcase. At the end of the corridor, a voice hails him.

DEPARTMENT HEAD
Van Hasebroeck! Are you leaving?

Thomas turns round.

I've found you another office. Room 305.

THOMAS
(*without looking at him*)
Well . . . I'd rather not switch offices.

DEPARTMENT HEAD
There'll be more light . . . your present window looks out on to a blank wall.

THOMAS
I know, I like my wall . . . It suits me.

The Department Head looks at Thomas in astonishment.

Oh, yes . . . I'd like some time off.

They stare at each other in silence for a moment. Suddenly, Thomas turns on his heels and leaves.

EXT. CEMETERY. DAY

A coffin is lowered into the ground. There are not many people present. Thomas stands beside adult Célestin. He looks gentle, almost angelic. His forehead is showing signs of baldness.

Thomas and Célestin move away. Beside the new grave, there are two older ones. The first is inscribed ARMAND VAN HASEBROECK. *It bears a photograph of the father. The other is inscribed* ALICE VAN HASEBROECK. *They walk towards the gates of the cemetery.*

> CÉLESTIN

So now there's just the two of us.

> THOMAS

Yes . . .

INT. CAR. DAY

Thomas is driving. Célestin looks out at the landscape.

> CÉLESTIN

What time is it?

> THOMAS
> (*glances at his watch*)

3.08 p.m.

> CÉLESTIN

Is that Daddy's watch?

> THOMAS

Yes.

Pause.

I hadn't seen Mum since . . . It's so stupid. I would have liked to see her one more time.

Célestin does not reply.

> CÉLESTIN

What time is it?

Thomas glances at his watch.

> THOMAS

3.09 p.m.

> CÉLESTIN

I have to be back at 4.

> THOMAS

We've got plenty of time.

> CÉLESTIN

Are you asking me what the time is?

> THOMAS

It's nine minutes past three.

> CÉLESTIN

No, you ask. Ask what time it is.

> THOMAS

Why?

> CÉLESTIN

You'll see.

> THOMAS

I know what time it is.

> CÉLESTIN

Ask me!

> THOMAS

Ok, what time is it?

Célestin waits for it.

> CÉLESTIN

The same time it was yesterday at the same time.

Célestin bursts out laughing. He laughs at the face Thomas is making. Thomas has to force a smile. Célestin watches him carefully.

You didn't get it, did you?

EXT. GATES OF AN INSTITUTE FOR THE MENTALLY
HANDICAPPED. DAY

*Thomas's car approaches a white building set in grounds. A nun
wearing a nurse's uniform walks by at the head of a small group of
mentally handicapped patients.*

CÉLESTIN
Stop here.

Thomas stops the car outside the gates. He switches the engine off.

How much time do we have left?

Thomas checks his watch.

THOMAS
Two minutes.

CÉLESTIN
Two minutes left.

They wait without talking . . .

*They get out of the car. Thomas takes his brother by the shoulder and
accompanies him to the gate. They pause.*

A kiss.

Thomas gives his brother a hug and kisses him.

What will you do?

THOMAS
I don't know. I need a change.

*Célestin strokes Thomas's face as though in consolation and walks off
towards the institute.*

CÉLESTIN
Watch out for ants!

THOMAS
Ants?

Célestin disappears. Thomas returns to his car and treads on an ant hill.

Shit!

Panic-stricken red ants run frantically around the sole of his shoe.

INT. BAR. DAY

Thomas is sitting in a dark bar finishing off a glass of whisky. He looks lost. He is watching a football game on TV.

A voice behind him.

Thomas!

Thomas turns round. At a table in a corner, a Man of about thirty is staring at him with a smile. He seems somewhat the worse for wear. Thomas does not recognize him. The Man chuckles.

MAN
Hey! Don't you know who I am?

Thomas tries to recognize the features.

Alfred.

Thomas cannot believe it.

Sit down for a sec!

Thomas does as he is told. For a long while they look at each other without saying a word. Thomas notices he is missing a button at his cuff which annoys him in front of Alfred.

Pause.

Well? Can't you think of anything to say?

THOMAS
You haven't said anything either . . .

ALFRED
Won't you ask me how I am?

Thomas says nothing.

Drunk as a lord and much wealthier, thanks to Daddy! Ha
ha!

Silence.

Where have you been all this time?

THOMAS

Here. I haven't moved.

ALFRED

Amazing we've never bumped into each other. We must not
move in the same circles.

THOMAS

I don't go out much.

ALFRED

Let me guess. You're married with two children and you go
to Spain every year for your holidays.

THOMAS

I'm not married and I spend my holidays here.

ALFRED

And why not?

Alfred scrutinizes Thomas.

Remember when we were kids, you wanted to swap your life
for mine?

THOMAS

I like my life.

He picks up his coat.

ALFRED

Of the two of us, you got the best deal. All right then . . . Van
Chickensoup.

Thomas gets to his feet. Alfred hands him a visiting card.

Here's my card. If there's ever anything your old friend can
do for you . . .

Thomas takes the card and leaves the bar. On the threshold, he tears it up. We stay on Alfred, who smiles as he watches Thomas go off.

> OLD THOMAS
> (*voice-over*)
> Vanish! You don't exist! I can't remember you! You're dead!

Alfred stands and goes to the door.

EXT. 'LES ROSES' VILLA. NIGHT

The corpse in its body-bag is carried through the door by two stretcher-bearers and slid onto a waiting ambulance. The ambulance door slams shut. It drives off.

INT. ROOM IN A RETIREMENT HOME. NIGHT

Old Thomas's face. He turns in bed. He can't sleep. He is in a sweat.

EXT. THOMAS'S STREET. DAY

Young Thomas walks into the house carrying a heavy shopping bag. From behind the fence of his garden, Alfred watches him.

> ALFRED
> Hey! Van Chickensoup!

> THOMAS
> My name isn't Van Chickensoup.

> ALFRED
> Van Chickensoup, is it true your father dropped into the sea and was swallowed up by fish?

Thomas closes his front door.

INT. PARENTS' BEDROOM. DAY

Goldfish swim around an aquarium. A small plaster diver bubbles away at the bottom. From behind the greenish glass, Thomas watches the fish. Sound of pump and bubbles bursting at the surface. Thomas pours in a little food. The fish rush to devour it.

In the background, the Mother is lying in bed. Célestin lies beside her. Alice removes a food tray.

> ALICE
>
> You've hardly eaten anything.

> MOTHER
>
> I'm not hungry.

> ALICE
>
> Have half, at least.

The Mother sighs like a little girl. She rolls on to her side.

> MOTHER
>
> I'm going to sleep. Make sure Thomas and Célestin don't go to bed too late.

She brushes Alice's cheek, then Thomas's. The children leave the room.

INT. LIVING-ROOM. NIGHT

The living-room is dark. Alice slips some film into an 8mm projector. She starts it. Alice and Thomas are huddled up together, fascinated by the flickering 8mm images of faces lit up. Célestin is half-asleep on the couch.

EXT. 8MM IMAGES, AIRPORT. DAY

On the wall, a succession of images . . . the Father climbs into an aeroplane and waves goodbye at the camera.

EXT. 8MM IMAGES, THOMAS'S GARDEN. DAY

The Father with a smile, Alice throwing a ball up into the air, the Mother laughing . . . the Father washing his car . . . the Father performing a magic trick to camera: a sweet vanishes. The images are not particularly meaningful, badly shot, full of uneventful passages and unsuccessful sequences.

INT. LIVING-ROOM. NIGHT

Thomas and Alice watch with fascination, in religious silence. Thomas gets up and goes to the piano. He stares at the keys, gently strokes them, presses one: the piano is out of tune.

INT. THOMAS'S ROOM. NIGHT

*Young Thomas in bed, eyes open, staring up at the ceiling. The hum of
a plane coming closer. The tooth-glass tinkles on the washbasin.
Thomas puts his pillow over his head. The sound of the plane moves
away. The door opens. Alice comes in. She sits on the edge of Thomas's
bed. They look at each other. Thomas starts to cry.*

> ALICE
>
> Would you . . . would you rather we said Daddy is dead and
> never coming back? Do you think that would be better?

Thomas shakes his head. Alice slips into his bed. She hugs him.
> (*Whispering*)
>
> I can hear your heart.

*A quiet thud. Alice puts her ear to Thomas's chest. She lifts up his
pyjama top and puts her ear to his tummy. A rumbling sound. Alice
laughs. She takes hold of Thomas and makes him roll over her. They
look at each other and burst out laughing. Alice takes his head in her
hands and kisses him on the mouth. Thomas dares not move. They
grow very serious.*

> Do you know what, Thomas?

> THOMAS
>
> My name's not Thomas!

> ALICE
>
> What is it, then?

> THOMAS
>
> Toto.

Toto aims his finger like a gun . . .

EXT. THOMAS'S STREET. NIGHT

*Toto repeats the same gesture: he aims his gun. The doors of the
gangsters' Jag slam shut and the car drives off. Toto shoots at them.*

> OLD THOMAS
> (*voice-over*)
>
> Bang bang!

The car vanishes round a corner. Toto jumps in his car and takes off after them.

EXT. 'LES ROSES' VILLA STREET. NIGHT

Toto drives hell for leather down a deserted street. He slams on the brakes and goes into reverse. He opens the door and sees something glint on the ground by the entrance to a garden: it's a sweet-wrapper. Toto looks up at the house. The gangsters' Jag is parked at the top of a drive, outside a mansion. The ground-floor windows are all lit up. A voice reaches us.

FATHER
(voice-over; in the distance)

Glug-glug-glug go the turkeys. And the lovely bell rings ding-a-ling-ding.

Toto brandishes his revolver and goes up the drive towards the Jag.

EXT. KANT SUPERMARKET. DAY

Mr Kant's Jaguar is parked outside a supermarket. Across the road, Young Thomas, his Mother, Alice and Célestin are staring at it. Band music.

Twenty or so passers-by are gathered around the entrance to the supermarket. A small band is playing something cheerful. Mr Kant is on parade with a number of official-looking people. He cuts a ribbon. Applause. The group enters the supermarket.

INT. KANT SUPERMARKET. DAY

Thomas's Mother enters the supermarket, followed by her children. Everything is gleaming and new and 'American-style'. Thomas's Mother spots Mr Kant being photographed in front of a stack of cans, with his wife and Alfred. He goes back to the cluster of official-looking people. Thomas's Mother clutches at his sleeve.

MOTHER

Mr Kant!

Mr Kant is obviously put out at the sight of her.

I . . . excuse me . . . I've had no news of husband . . . No one's told me anything . . .

MR KANT

Now's not a good time . . . and anyway, I know no more than you do. Go home, wait and be patient.

He tries to go about his business. Thomas's Mother retains him, holding his sleeve tightly.

MOTHER
(*irritated*)

How can I possibly wait and be patient?

She won't let go of his sleeve.

MR KANT

Please let go of me.

ALFRED

Leave Daddy alone!

Alfred shoves Thomas's Mother away. She slaps him. Alfred hides in his mother's skirts.

MR KANT

Madam, please! Calm down!

Thomas's Mother hides her face in her hands and cries. Thomas and Alice approach. Mr Kant takes Thomas's Mother aside.

Listen. I'm not responsible for what may have happened to your husband. I asked him to go to England to fetch some goods in time for the opening of my shop, that's all. I did not ask him to take unacceptable risks.

MOTHER

You asked him to take off during a storm!

MR KANT

Your husband accepted. I wasn't asking for heroics, I only wanted him to transport some goods for me.

MOTHER

What goods?

Mr Kant hesitates. He is somewhat embarrassed to have to admit . . .

MR KANT

Marmalade.

The Mother's face creases up in pain.

INT. CHURCH. DAY

A tearful Holy Virgin. The heavy door opens with a crash. Alice enters the deserted church, dragging Thomas behind her.

ALICE

We've come to warn you . . . if they don't find our daddy, you're going to pay for it. Something awful will happen. Mr Kant, you, everyone's going to pay! So they'd better find him fast or else . . .

She waves her fist at the statue.

EXT. RAILWAY BRIDGE. DAY

Thomas and Célestin walk down a country path beside a field of cows. They come to a railway bridge where a bunch of kids about their age are playing at throwing knives. Thomas recognizes Alfred, who glares at him.

ONE OF THE KIDS

There's Van Chickensoup and his loony brother.

THOMAS

My name's not Van Chickensoup.

ANOTHER KID

Is it true your mother slapped Alfred?

ALFRED

Cut it out!

The gang surrounds Thomas. They jeer at Célestin. Célestin smiles back. The toughest of the kids comes up to Célestin.

TOUGH KID

I hear you fly like a bird? Alfred saw you when you were about the fly out of the window.

163

The kids all think this is funny. Thomas stares at Alfred with loathing. The place is deserted. The Tough Kid climbs on to the parapet, fifty feet above the tracks. He turns to Célestin.

Go on! Show us! Fly off over there, then go between those two posts and come back here, OK?

They all burst out laughing. Two kids push Célestin towards the wall. Thomas tries to intervene. Two other kids grab him by the waist.

THOMAS

Leave him alone!

Célestin climbs up on to parapet. He looks up at the sky. He spreads his arms slowly. He fills his lungs with air. A gust of wind blows through his hair and billows his shirt out. He leans forwards a fraction.

Célestin! No!

Alfred thumps Thomas in the solar plexus, winding him. Célestin remains as though suspended above the void, with his arms spread.

ALFRED

Go on! Fly!

THOMAS

Not the birdy, Célestin! Do something else!

A cow moos in the field. Célestin turns to it. He looks back at the boys and points two fingers above his head like two horns.

CÉLESTIN

Moooooo!

The kids like this. They imitate him.

KIDS

Mooooooo! Mooooooo! Ha ha ha!

Célestin imitates a bull, pushing his 'horns' forward. He charges head first into the Tough Kid's belly so the Tough Kid is sent flying several yards. The others watch in amazement. Alfred is thrown against the parapet. He runs off, with the others in pursuit. Thomas is on the ground. Célestin helps him up. Thomas sees his brother in a new light. Célestin runs away, arms spread, as though he is about to take off.

INT. LIVING-ROOM. DAY

Thomas is doing his homework on the dining-room table. Célestin is drawing at the same table. Alice, wearing a blue dress, leaves the house carrying a trumpet in its case.

THOMAS

Where are you going?

ALICE

Mind your own business . . . Mum, I'm off to my music lesson.

She slams the door. In the back of the room, the Mother is on the phone. Her hair is not combed. She is smoking a cigarette. A newspaper is open in front of her.

MOTHER

The vacancy's been filled, has it? Oh . . . I'm sorry . . .

Somewhat put out, she hangs up and dials another number.

I'm calling about the ad for a waitress. I . . . no, I don't really have any experience but I . . .

Thomas is watching his Mother. She is not aware of him. He takes two coins out of his pocket and, without her noticing, slips them into his mother's handbag, which is hanging on a nearby chair.

INT. KANT SUPERMARKET, CHECK-OUT. DAY

A few coins beside a bottle of milk and some cans. The Mother, wearing a hat, is at the check-out with Alice, Thomas and Célestin.

Suddenly, the cashier yells. Blood dribbles down on to the mother's face from her hair. The mother realizes what is happening and turns pale.

CASHIER

Excuse me? Are you all right? Shall I get a doctor?

People gather round the Mother. They try to get her to sit down.

MOTHER

No, I'm . . . I'm fine. It's nothing.

Her face is covered in blood. Mr Kant pushes his way through the small crowd to find out what is going on. He leans over the Mother.

MR KANT

Call an ambulance!

Mr Kant removes the mother's hat. Suddenly, the crowd falls silent. Under the hat, there is a large piece of steak bleeding into her hair. Everyone stares at the meat, petrified. The mother lowers her eyes in shame. Faces turn and stare at the children. Thomas blushes.

INT. CHURCH. DAY

Alice stops at the foot of the Holy Virgin. Thomas joins her.

ALICE

We warned you!

She pushes the base of the statue. It topples and shatters in a cloud of white dust.

INT. KANT SUPERMARKET. DAY

Mr Kant is watching a poster go up above a stack of pots of marmalade. Alice observes him. She drags Thomas in between two rows of shelving. She signals that he is to wait.

Alice wanders through the beauty products and takes a tube of lipstick, which she tries out on the back of her hand. A Sales Assistant has seen her. She takes a pair of silk tights and slips them under her jumper. The Sales Assistant watches. She adds a comic, a bottle of scent and a box of matches. She goes to the back of the shop and enters the toilet. The Sales Assistant runs to warn Mr Kant.

INT. SUPERMARKET TOILET. DAY

Alice locks the cubicle. She lifts up her jumper and lets all the things she's taken drop into the washbasin. She tears up the comic, lights a match and throws it in.

INT. SUPERMARKET. DAY

Alice walks past the check-out tills without stopping. The Sales Assistant is waiting for her. He takes her by the shoulder.

> SALES ASSISTANT
> One moment, miss! What have you got there?

Mr Kant joins them. The Sales Assistant lifts up Alice's jumper. There's nothing underneath except for Alice's bare chest. Alice yells at Mr Kant as loud as she possibly can.

> ALICE
> You must be out of your mind! You filthy old man! Get your hands off me!

People stop and look. Mr Kant doesn't know what to do.

> MR KANT
> I'm sorry, miss, I . . .

Alice readjusts her clothes, insulting him for all she's worth.

> ALICE
> What were you after? You bastard! You pervert! You lecherous old man!

Mr Kant sheepishly watches her leave. At the back of the shop, someone shouts, 'Fire!'

Smoke billows out of the toilets. Mr Kant rushes over. The Sales Assistant appears with a fire extinguisher. He opens the door, points the fire extinguisher in the right direction and presses down on the handle. Everything goes still. Nothing happens. Mr Kant grabs the fire extinguisher, directs it and presses down on the handle. Everything goes still. Nothing happens. A cashier comes with a bucket of water.

EXT. KANT SUPERMARKET. DAY

Alice and Thomas watch the entrance. Alice thinks this is funny but Thomas is in a panic.

> ALICE
>
> Brilliant! That's what we'll do.

> THOMAS
>
> What?

EXT. THOMAS'S STREET. DAY

Alice skips home. Thomas follows uncomfortably.

> THOMAS
>
> What will we do?

> ALICE
>
> Go to Kant's and set fire to his house.

Thomas stares at Alice with terror.

> THOMAS
>
> You're crazy! It's dangerous!

Alice stops and spins round.

> ALICE
>
> Crazy? Who's crazy?

> THOMAS
>
> You.

Alice laughs in his face. She turns her back on him, laughing harder and harder until her laughter turns to tears. She buries her face in her hands. Thomas tries to touch her shoulder. She shakes him off and runs away. Thomas tries to catch up with her.

Wait!

ALICE

Go away!

Eyes brimming with tears, Alice trips over. Thomas tries to catch her.

THOMAS

I can tell you where there's some petrol. In the garage.

ALICE

What do you want petrol for?

THOMAS

The fire . . .

ALICE

Bastards like you don't know anything about fires!

She goes inside and slams the door.

INT. THOMAS'S ROOM. DAWN

*Thomas wakes up. He hears something. Muffled steps in the corridor.
He gets up.*

INT. CORRIDOR AND PARENTS' ROOM. DAWN

*Through the half-open door, Thomas sees his Mother kneeling at the
wardrobe in a towelling dressing-gown. She takes the father's shoes and
puts them in a cardboard box. She wraps up the father's clothes. She
stops to caress a shirt. Thomas cannot believe his eyes. He moves back
silently. Suddenly the phone rings downstairs. The Mother turns round.
She sees Thomas. They are equally surprised. After a moment, the
Mother leaves the room and goes downstairs.*

INT. LIVING-ROOM (CURTAINS CLOSED). DAWN

The Mother switches the lights on and answers the phone.

MOTHER

Hello? Yes?

She listens. What she hears transforms her.

169

Thomas comes downstairs. Alice is behind him in her nightgown.

The Mother hangs up. She sees them. Her lips tremble. She tries to contain herself.

> ALICE
>
> Have they found Daddy?

> MOTHER
>
> His plane.

> ALICE
>
> What about him?

> MOTHER
>
> They don't know yet. Someone called from Dover.

> ALICE
>
> Will you go there?

> MOTHER
>
> I . . .

> ALICE
>
> You've got to!

> MOTHER
>
> What would I do with you?

> ALICE
>
> Take Célestin with you. We'll go to summer camp.

> MOTHER
>
> You hate summer camp.

> ALICE
>
> That isn't true! I like it.

INT. ALICE'S ROOM. NIGHT

A suitcase on the bed. The Mother, wearing a coat, finishes packing Alice's clothes.

> MOTHER
>
> There, that should do. The camp bus will come by tomorrow morning. Don't miss it!

She takes a little money out of her bag and gives it to Alice. Someone hoots in the street outside.

> ALICE

Your taxi!

Thomas's Mother gives him a hug then she smothers Alice in kisses.

EXT. THOMAS'S STREET (POV: WINDOW). NIGHT

The Mother climbs into a taxi with Célestin. The taxi drives off.

INT. THOMAS'S ROOM. DAY

Thomas finishes dressing. His case is ready.

INT. ALICE'S ROOM. DAY

Thomas walks into Alice's room and stops, speechless. The case is on the bed, empty. The clothes have been put back in the cupboard.

> THOMAS

Alice!? Alice!!

INT. BATHROOM. DAY

Thomas pushes the bathroom door.

> THOMAS

Alice?

Alice is lying in the bath, up to her neck in foam. She opens her eyes slightly, sees Thomas and shuts her eyes again, relaxing in the water.

That's Mummy's bubblebath. You're not supposed to use it.

> ALICE

Really? I can't believe you're saying that!

She sinks back into the water deliciously. Thomas does not know what to do.

> THOMAS

Why have you unpacked? We'll be late for the bus.

Because we're not going.

THOMAS
What?

ALICE
We're staying here. Hand me a bath towel.

Alice stands in the bath. Thomas looks her up and down.

Have you gone deaf? Hand me a bath towel.

Thomas takes a towel. Clumsily, he lets it drop, picks it up, then gives it to Alice, blushing.

THOMAS
You didn't say you had breasts now.

ALICE
Oh, sorry. I thought you'd seen it in the papers.

THOMAS
Why? Was it in the papers?

Alice looks at Thomas with something like pity.

ALICE
Poor Thomas.

Thomas blushes.

Is something the matter? Don't you want to stay?

Thomas backs out of the bathroom.

THOMAS
Me? Er, no. No problem . . .

He blushes again and shuts the door.

EXT. THOMAS'S STREET (POV: LIVING-ROOM). DAY

A horn blows. Through the closed shutters, a bus is seen stopping in the street outside the house. The driver gets out and walks towards the house.

INT. LIVING-ROOM (SHUTTERS CLOSED). DAY

Thomas and Alice peek through the shutters. the house is in semi-darkness. They crouch down and hide on the floor against the wall. The doorbell rings. They exchange a look. Pause. Another ring. They exchange another look. Alice smothers a giggle.

THOMAS

Ssshhh!

Alice tries to stop herself laughing. Thomas has hiccups. Alice bursts out laughing, with her hands pressed against her mouth. Steps on the gravel. Sound of the bus starting up and driving off.

They burst out laughing. Alice gives Thomas a hug. They roll around on the floor and come to a stop, clasped in each other's arms. There is a moment's silence. Then they whisper.

What'll we do if Mummy doesn't come back?

ALICE

We'll carry on like this. We won't tell anyone anything.

THOMAS

And stay here? Just the two of us?

ALICE

We'll always be together. After the holidays, we won't go back to school. I won't go to my trumpet lessons any more.

THOMAS

What if someone finds out Mummy isn't here?

ALICE

We could set fire to the house and run away. Everyone would think we were dead, but we'd be alive. We'd go miles away and no one would ever find out.

Thomas looks worried. Alice watches him.

Nobody will know Mummy isn't here. It's our secret.

EXT. THOMAS'S STREET. DAY

Thomas is dragging a shopping bag that is much too heavy. He turns around and speeds up. He goes round a corner. He looks round again. Alfred is after him. Thomas goes as fast as he can. He walks faster and faster. Suddenly, Alfred's hand takes the bag out of his hands. Thomas jumps.

ALFRED

Here. I'll take it.

Thomas doesn't dare contradict him. Alfred walks along beside him.

Why didn't you go to camp?

THOMAS

What?

ALFRED

The bus came for you. Why didn't you go?

Thomas says nothing. He has reached his house. Alfred comes right to the door. Thomas takes the bag back. Alfred waits expectantly. Thomas opens the door and slips inside.

INT. LIVING-ROOM. DAY

Alfred forces his way inside. He glances around. Breakfast is strewn over the table. Milk drips off the table. Clothes lie over the furniture.

ALFRED

Is your mother in?

THOMAS

Yes.

ALFRED

I doubt it. She'd clean up.

THOMAS

I told you. She's here.

ALFRED

I bet she isn't. I bet she doesn't even know you didn't go. Mrs Van Hasebroeck? Mrs Van Hasebroeck!

Alice appears behind Thomas.

ALICE

Mummy's ill in bed. Do you want to speak to her?

Alfred's attitude changes on seeing Alice.

ALFRED

Errr . . .

ALICE

I'll let her know! (*She turns to the stairs and shouts out.*)
Mummy!

She runs up the stairs. Thomas watches her with surprise. Alice can be heard talking to someone upstairs, then she comes down.

She can't come down right now. The doctor has told her not
to get out of bed.

ALFRED

It's . . . it's nothing, I . . . It doesn't matter . . . all right.

ALICE

Thank you for coming round.

ALFRED

Right, well . . .

ALICE

Bye.

She shuts the door on Alfred, then lets out a sigh of relief. Thomas looks at her with concern.

THOMAS

Do you think he noticed anything?

INT. THOMAS'S ROOM. NIGHT

Thomas and Alice are in Thomas's bed, lying side by side. Alice blows a saliva bubble on her lips. She runs a finger down the ridge of her nose.

ALICE
(*whispering*)

Do you like my nose?

THOMAS

Yes.

Pause.

ALICE

Don't you think I look like a boy?

THOMAS

No . . .

ALICE

Don't you think my legs are like a grasshopper's?

THOMAS

No . . .

ALICE

Are you sure?

THOMAS

Yes!

Alice watches her hands against the ceiling.

Are my hands nice? Which do you think is the nicest?

THOMAS

They're both nice.

ALICE

But which do you like best?

THOMAS

I like them both best.

ALICE

And what about my mark? You don't think it's ugly?

She displays a birthmark on her belly, just beside the belly-button. Thomas kisses the birthmark. He spits on to it and rubs. Alice laughs.

It doesn't wash off, you idiot! Hi hi!

She kisses the top of Thomas's head, then produces one of her feet out from under the sheets and examines it.

And my feet? They're not too big, are they?

Thomas sighs. He buries himself against Alice and softly dares a hand against her breast. He looks at her. She lets him.

THOMAS

Do you know what? Nefertiti was queen of Egypt.

ALICE

Well? So what?

THOMAS

She got married to her brother. In Egypt, that's allowed.

Alice gives Thomas a look. She bursts out laughing. She hugs Thomas's head. Thomas looks up. On the table he sees an artificial flower, with some scissors, glue and cloth.

What's that?

ALICE

It's a flower. I made it.

When?

ALICE

When you weren't looking.

Thomas gets up to take it. She prevents him.

THOMAS

Is it . . . is it for me?

Alice laughs.

Can I see it?

ALICE

Later . . .

She puts the flower in a drawer.

INT. ALICE'S ROOM. DAY

Alice examines herself in the mirror. She puts on a blue and white dress. Thomas buttons up the back. Her hair is long at the back and held in a yellow clasp.

She puts lipstick on.

THOMAS

What are you doing?

Alice presses her lips against a handkerchief. Thomas stares uneasily at her reflection. She is not the same, she looks grown-up.

ALICE

How old would you say I was?

Thomas doesn't know what to reply. He is overcome. Alice picks up her music bag and gets ready to go. Thomas does not understand why she is in such a hurry.

THOMAS

Where are you going?

ALICE

To my trumpet lesson.

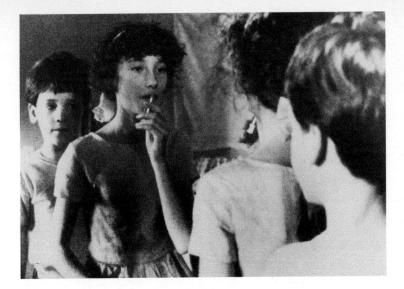

character
THOMAS
I thought you weren't going any more.

She leaves. Thomas is curious.

EXT. STREET. DAY

Alice treads lightly up the street. Thomas follows at a respectable distance, trying not to be seen.

EXT. LEVEL-CROSSING. DAY

Alice walks over the level-crossing. The barrier comes down. Thomas has to stop as a goods train goes by. It's a slow train. Thomas tries to see through it. The train keeps on blocking his view and he sees what Alice is up to only intermittently. He sees that she is waiting . . . He sees Alfred join her. She chats to him. Alfred is all smiles. At one point, Alice's hand touches Alfred's. Thomas goes pale. The last coaches go by. The barrier rises. On the other side, there is no one left. Thomas's jaw drops.

EXT. FOOTBALL GROUND. DAY

*Noise, hooting, rattles. Adult Thomas is at a football match. He seems
tired and is irritated by his neighbour's cigarette smoke.*

>   THOMAS
> Do you know, 60 per cent of all cancers are caused by
> cigarette smoke?

*The smoker glares at him aggressively. He looks a brute. Thomas falls
silent. His mind wanders from the match. He looks at the crowd.
Something attracts his notice: a head of brown hair . . . Thomas strains
to get a better view . . . About twenty yards below, a dark woman
wearing a 1950s-style blue and white dress . . . The hairstyle, dress and
hairband are the same as Alice used to wear. People block his view.
Thomas has a split-second vision of child Alice. He stands. People try to
get him to sit down. At last, he sees the woman's face. She's about thirty
and looks only vaguely like Alice. Thomas stares at her. The referee
blows his whistle. Everyone stands and cheers. The woman is hidden
from view.*

> Alice!

People leave their seats. Thomas has lost her.

EXT. FOOTBALL GROUND EXITS. DAY

*Thomas tries to fight his way through the crowd clustered around the
exits. He shoves people out of the way. Again, he loses sight of the
woman. He moves as fast as he can but there are too many people in the
way. One fan grabs him. Thomas tries to wriggle free. His collar tears.
Thomas runs off, leaving his collar in his attacker's hand.*

EXT. OUTSIDE THE FOOTBALL GROUND. DAY

*Thomas bursts out of the stadium, exhausted. He looks around. The
crowd is dispersing. Thomas sees only unfamiliar faces. He sighs and
stands frozen in a sea of tarmac littered with greasy wastepaper. The
crowd disperses completely. He remains alone.*

EXT. CEMETERY. DAY

Thomas enters the cemetery in which his Mother was buried. A motorway straddles the graveyard. *He knows the way. He comes to his mother's tomb. The earth is still freshly turned over. On one side, a grave with his father's portrait. Next door, a tomb marked:*

ALICE VAN HASEBROECK

9.6.53   13.7.64

Thomas takes a deep breath. There is a china photograph of Alice on the tomb, wearing the blue and white dress and hairband. The face itself is hardly visible. The hooting of a truck on the motorway. Thomas stares at the photograph.

EXT. LEVEL-CROSSING. DAY

Hooting of a train as it goes by. Alice in her blue and white dress. She smiles at Alfred. The bell at the level-crossing rings. Young Thomas's face through the carriages. Thomas runs away.

EXT. FIELDS. DAY

Thomas cries as he runs down a country path beside the railway line. From the far side of a fence, cows watch him go by. Thomas picks up a clod of earth and chucks it at them.

THOMAS

Stop staring at me!

INT. LIVING-ROOM. DAY

Thomas comes into the house. Alice's laughter fills the room. Thomas is by the door, dumbstruck. Alfred is in one of the armchairs. He looks at Thomas. Alice stops laughing. Thomas is livid. Alice tries to conceal her embarrassment.

ALICE

(*to Thomas*)

Alfred knows a brilliant riddle . . . (*to Alfred*) Tell him!

ALFRED

What's green and –

Alice is laughing already. Thomas turns on his heels and climbs the stairs four at a time.

181

INT. THOMAS'S ROOM. DAY

Thomas is lying face down on his bed, turned to the wall. Alice opens the door.

> ALICE
>
> What's wrong with you?

> THOMAS
>
> You're out of your mind! We're supposed to have a secret.

> ALICE
>
> I didn't tell him anything.

> THOMAS
>
> He'll soon guess Mummy isn't here.

> ALICE
>
> Even if he does, he won't tell. I know he won't.

> THOMAS
>
> You're mad!

Thomas pushes Alice out of his room and locks the door. Alice drums at the door. Thomas collapses on to his bed in despair. He hears them talking downstairs. The front door slams. Thomas looks out of the window.

EXT. THOMAS'S (POV: WINDOW) STREET. DAY

Alfred walks away. He is alone.

EXT. RAILWAY BRIDGE. EVENING

Thomas is hidden in bushes watching Alfred and his gang chucking knives.

> KID'S VOICE
>
> HEY! VAN CHICKENSOUP'S SPYING ON US!

Thomas is startled. Two kids grab him from behind. They twist his arm and drag him into the middle of the group.

> ALFRED
>
> What are you following me for?

Thomas says nothing.

ONE OF THE KIDS

Maybe he wants a go with the knife.

ALFRED

Get out of here.

ONE OF THE KIDS

Are you scared he could beat you?

Alfred is put out. He pulls a knife out of the target and offers it to Thomas. The others shove him into the middle of the group and put the knife in his hand. Thomas has no idea how to hold it.

KIDS
(chanting)

VAN-CHI-CKEN-SOUP-VAN-CHI-CKEN-SOUP . . .

Thomas throws the knife. It lands almost bang in the bull's-eye. Thomas is surprised. Alfred is furious. He takes the knife, throws it. It bounces off the target. One of the kids bursts out laughing. Alfred is beside himself with rage. He picks up the knife and moves towards Thomas. Thomas pushes the kids out of the way and runs off.

EXT. WOODS. DUSK

Thomas runs down a narrow path through the woods. It is almost dark. Sound of running behind him. Thomas turns round. At the end of the path, he sees the shape of Alfred. Thomas runs faster. Branches scratch his face. Alfred is gaining on him. Thomas slips in a puddle and falls into a stream. He can hear Alfred's steps growing closer. Thomas lies down in the stream, without breathing so as not to make any noise. He is half out of the water. He dares not look up. Thomas holds his breath. Alfred looks around.

ALFRED

THOMAS!

He can't see him. Thomas does not budge, does not breathe.

COME BACK! I WON'T HURT YOU!

Thomas sees something glint in Alfred's hand: the blade. Thomas buries

183

himself as deep as he can in the water. He hears Alfred's voice.

Shit!

Alfred throws the knife up in the air. It describes an arc and falls with a splash into the stream three feet away from Thomas. Alfred goes away.

Thomas remains in the water without moving. Forest sounds return. At last he has the courage to get out of the water. The blade glints in the water.

INT. RETIREMENT HOME CORRIDOR AND LODGE. NIGHT

The doorkeeper's gun is in the drawer. Old Thomas is hidden in the corner. He grasps his coat and case. It is dark. Everything seems to be sleeping. Thomas watches the doorkeeper leave his lodge and move off. Thomas rushes forward. He opens the drawer, takes the gun and slips it into his pocket. He takes a key. On a security screen, Thomas sees the doorkeeper coming back. Thomas rips a bit of aluminium chocolate wrapper, switches the desklight off, unscrews the bulb, pushes the foil into the socket and screws the bulb back in.

INT. RETIREMENT HOME EXIT. NIGHT

Thomas appears. He is out of breath. He looks up at the surveillance camera aimed at the exit. The red light is on.

INT. LODGE. NIGHT

The doorkeeper sits down. He notices the light is off and switches it on, shorting the circuit. The lamp fizzles. The fuses go. All the lights go out. The image on the security monitors disappears. The doorkeeper swears.

INT. RETIREMENT HOME EXIT. NIGHT

The lights are out. The red light on the camera goes out. Thomas makes a run for the door and slips the key in the lock. A sound. Thomas looks round. An old man is watching him. Thomas puts a finger to his lips and says, 'Sssh.' The old man puts two fingers to his lips, meaning 'Cigarette.' Thomas tosses him a few cigarettes. He opens the door and escapes.

EXT. WOOD. NIGHT

Alfred's knife glinting in the water.

INT. LIVING-ROOM. NIGHT

Young Thomas enters the house, soaked to the skin. Mud and blood on his face. Alice screams with fright. Thomas cries with rage.

ALICE

What happened to you?

THOMAS

You were going to set fire to their house, but you've forgotten already.

ALICE

Thomas, what's going on?

THOMAS

You're in love with Alfred! You lied to me! You're like everyone else! You'll never set fire to it!

Alice is dismayed.

ALICE

Who did that to you?

THOMAS

It's OK for you to be in love with him, but not with me because I'm your brother.

She takes his head in her hands.

ALICE

Thomas! You're crazy! I am in love with you! I don't care you're my brother. You're the one I'm in love with.

THOMAS

WELL, WHY WON'T YOU SET FIRE TO HIS HOUSE, THEN? EH?

Alice looks him in the eye.

ALICE

Is that what you want? Is it?

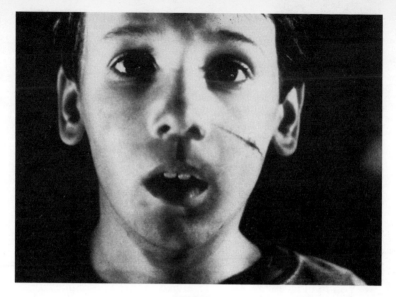

THOMAS
YOU'LL NEVER DO IT!

ALICE
Will you believe me if I do?

Thomas shoves Alice away and runs to hide in his room.

INT. THOMAS'S ROOM. NIGHT

Thomas is sobbing into his bed. A noise in the street. Thomas gets up and goes to the window . . . His eyes open wide.

EXT. THOMAS'S STREET (POV: WINDOW). NIGHT

Downstairs, in the street, Alice, carrying a petrol can towards the Kant family warehouse. The petrol can makes a dull thudding sound against the tarmac . . .

EXT. KANT GARDEN. NIGHT

Alice walking up to the hangar, dragging the petrol can along the ground. She breaks a window-pane.

INT. LIVING-ROOM. NIGHT

Thomas runs down the stairs as fast as he can.

> THOMAS
> (*screaming*)

ALICE!!

EXT. THOMAS'S STREET AND KANT GARDEN. NIGHT

Thomas runs out of the house and up to the hangar.

> THOMAS
> (*shouting*)

ALICE!!

He reaches the middle of the street. A flame shows in the middle of the hangar, when suddenly . . .

EXT. MODEL (POV: THOMAS). NIGHT

. . . an explosion blows the door off the hangar. The windows shatter.

EXT. THOMAS'S STREET AND KANT GARDEN. NIGHT

Thomas is petrified, his face all lit up by the fire. Flames climb up the corrugated-iron roofing, which twists with a bang. The petrol pump at the entrance to the hangar is belching out a great tongue of flame. Thomas stares wide-eyed.

EXT. THOMAS'S STREET. NIGHT

People come out of the neighbouring houses. An old couple put their furniture into the street. Police lights illuminate the houses. Mr Kant, in his pyjamas, stands in his garden beside his wife and Alfred. Firemen and policemen run in every direction. Alone, immobile despite all the commotion, Thomas stares into the flames. He is in a state of shock. Slowly, he moves towards the fire . . .

> THOMAS

Alice . . .

One of the firemen shoves him back.

ALICE!!

Alfred turns to Thomas and understands. Alfred's face breaks up. He stares into the flames and yells as loud as he can. His father picks him up and consoles him with a pat on the back.

MR KANT

Don't cry. We'll rebuild it.

Alfred struggles in his father's arms. He is yelling with pain. Thomas stares at the fire, petrified. Police and fire-engine lights strobe across his face.

INT. MORGUE CORRIDOR. NIGHT

Same rhythm: the regular pulse of neon lights somewhere above us. Pushed along on a metal stretcher, a corpse goes in and out of the light.

INT. MORGUE. NIGHT

The corpse comes to a halt under a bright light. The zip on the body-bag is pulled. Scissors cut into the clothes.

INT. LIVING-ROOM

The living-room is empty except for a few cardboard boxes. The Mother, red-eyed and dressed in black, holds Thomas and Célestin by the hand. They are in mourning too. They watch two removal men taking furniture out.

INT. HEADMASTER'S OFFICE, DAY

Playground noise. Thomas is seated beside his Mother in the Headmaster's office. The Headmaster is filling out a form. Thomas seems absent-minded and sad. The Headmaster looks up and smiles at him.

HEADMASTER

And what are we going to go in for?

Thomas sighs. His eyes wander over the walls. Pinned high on one of them is a poster marked BECOME A SURVEYOR. *Thomas turns to the Headmaster.*

188

THOMAS

Surveyor.

INT. THOMAS'S OFFICE. DAY

*Plans for a new bridge and new roads are pinned on the wall. Thomas
stands at his desk in a raincoat. He is unshaven. He shoves his
belongings into a cardboard box, including a photo of Alice as a child.
His Department Head is at his side, watching.*

DEPARTMENT HEAD

Van Hasebroeck, I don't understand. I think you're making a
mistake.

Thomas does not reply.

Take a few extra days off. Come back when you've had a rest . . .

THOMAS

I've been here too long. I'm very sorry. It's nothing to do with
you. It's . . . personal.

He takes his box and leaves.

DEPARTMENT HEAD

Van Hasebroeck!

EXT. FOOTBALL GROUND EXIT. DAY

*The area is deserted. It has been raining. Thomas waits. He is
unshaven. He is soaking wet.*

*The gates open . . . a few spectators emerge. Thomas stares at them. He
fails to recognize anyone. Suddenly, a dark-haired woman passes beside
him. He grabs her by the arm and turns her around: it's the wrong
woman. The woman breaks away, wondering what he wants.*

INT. TRAIN COMPARTMENT. NIGHT

*Rocked by the train, Old Thomas tries to get to sleep in the semi-
darkness of the compartment. He takes a tattered book out of his pocket
and opens it. It is very hot. The other passengers look striking. They sigh
and fan themselves. Their clothes look strange. Thomas's gun sticks out
of his pocket. He digs it back in.*

INT. THOMAS'S APARTMENT. DAY

The curtains are drawn. Adult Thomas watches 8mm film projected on to a wall.

EXT. 8MM FILM IMAGES, THOMAS'S GARDEN. DAY

Out of focus, shaky footage of Alice as a child, running around the garden and hiding. The film is scratchy and the celluloid shows through. Alice turns to the camera and vanishes in a flash.

INT. THOMAS'S APARTMENT. DAY

The film unspools. Thomas watches the white flickering rectangle on the wall.

EXT. LEVEL-CROSSING. DAY

A bell. Thomas stops his car at a level-crossing in town. A train passes by. Thomas looks through the carriages as they go past.

The other side of the tracks, through the carriages, Thomas sees a dark Woman in a blue and white dress. She's the Woman he saw at the football match. She stands in exactly the same position as Alice, twenty years earlier. The barrier goes up. The Woman crosses the tracks, coming towards Thomas. She passes his car without noticing it. Thomas cannot believe his eyes. He follows her with his gaze. She is carrying a musical instrument in a case under her arm: a trumpet.

Horns sound behind him. Thomas parks his car on the pavement and runs after her.

EXT. STREET. DAY

Thomas follows the Woman. She walks twenty feet ahead of him. He tries not to be seen.

INT. BUSY STREET. DAY

People seem to hurry along. The Woman walks by the shop windows. Thomas follows some thirty feet behind her. He accelerates. He sees her enter a shop.

INT./EXT. MUSIC SHOP. DAY

*Thomas stares through the window. The shop sells instruments, records,
scores. The woman opens her case and hands her trumpet to the
Assistant. Thomas pushes the door open. A bell draws attention to him.
Thomas pretends to be interested in a display of musical scores. The
Assistant examines the instrument.*

ASSISTANT

The piston's stuck.

*Thomas manoeuvres in such a way as to catch a glimpse of the
woman's face. She is beautiful. Her features are vaguely reminiscent of
Alice's. Thomas stares at her in fascination. Their eyes meet. Thomas
cannot look away. The Woman is intrigued. She looks away.*

Can I take your address?

*The Woman watches Thomas staring at her. She does not answer
immediately.*

The Assistant waits expectantly.

WOMAN

Evelyne Deschamps, 28 rue des Bouleaux.

Thomas has heard. The Woman leaves the shop without turning round.

EXT. 'LES ROSES' VILLA. NIGHT

*A suburban villa set in a lawn. The number '28' is illuminated. Thomas
is in his car with the lights off. There is a light in a ground-floor
window. Thomas is hesitating. Eventually, he decides to get out of his
car and walk up the drive towards the house. He stops outside it.
Suddenly, a car appears from behind the house. The headlights dazzle
him. Brakes squeal. Thomas is knocked over by the car. He tries to raise
his head. He is lying on the gravel. The woman, Evelyne, comes out of
the car in distress.*

EVELYNE

I'm so sorry. Are you OK?

THOMAS

I'm sorry, I didn't mean it.

191

Evelyne is taken aback. She helps him up. Thomas tries to make out her face.

THOMAS

Do you know me?

She looks at him.

EVELYNE

No. I'll get a doctor. Were you coming to see my husband?

THOMAS

No, I was coming to see you. We've met.

They exchange a look. Thomas's eyes look over the white dress, drinking it in. Evelyne checks that the buttons at her neck are properly done up.

EVELYNE

Get up.

She helps Thomas up by an arm. Thomas holds her by the hand. Time seems to pause. A passing car lights them up. They look at each other. Evelyne wonders what is going on. Thomas's hand touches her dress. She looks at Thomas.

Of course I know you . . . You were at the music shop.

THOMAS

I heard you give your address. I had to talk to you.

This makes Evelyne nervous.

EVELYNE

What do you want?

THOMAS

I . . . I just need to talk to you.

EVELYNE

What about?

THOMAS

About you.

EVELYNE

Who are you?

She removes her hand from Thomas's grasp.

THOMAS

I need to see you again.

EVELYNE

If I were you, I'd leave me alone. My husband's at home.

THOMAS

How old are you?

Evelyne stares at him.

EVELYNE

What's that to you?

THOMAS

I want to know who you are?

EVELYNE

Go and see a doctor. I'll pay.

THOMAS

Please! I just want to talk to you! How can I see you again?

He tries to take her by the arm. She struggles.

EVELYNE

Please . . . Leave me alone.

Thomas realizes that he has gone too far.

THOMAS

I . . . I didn't want to frighten you. I'm going now.

He backs off. Evelyne watches him go.

EVELYNE

Wait.

Thomas stops. They stare at each other.

Who are you?

She hesitates.

Tomorrow I've got a bit of time after my rehearsal.

EXT. CITY STREET. NIGHT

Old Thomas emerges from a subway. Sound of a train. He surfaces in a busy street, looks around. He seems a bit lost.

Above the roofs, enormous television screens block out the sky broadcasting commercials. Thomas walks along. A few strange vehicles drive down the street. Most of the pedestrians seem old. A few young people in garish costumes look out of place. Thomas watches them with surprised distaste. On the opposite pavement, a police car without wheels hovers over the pavement, topped by a blue light. Thomas comes to a stop. He recognizes a statue stuck in between two buildings.

EXT. CONCERT HALL SQUARE. DAY

The same statue in a spacious square. The sun is shining. Lovers kiss. Thomas and Evelyne walk by, side by side. They are heading towards the entrance to a concert hall. Evelyne is carrying her instrument case.

> EVELYNE
> You're a funny guy . . . What else do you want to know. I'm thirty-one, my parents are schoolteachers, I'm a musician. I'm married to a man who works too hard. But I love him very much.

> THOMAS
> Where were you brought up?

> EVELYNE
> In Calais. Do you know Calais?

> THOMAS
> No. Never been there.

> EVELYNE
> See?

> THOMAS
> What about your husband?

194

We met at a concert. It was love at first sight, when he saw me play. He knows nothing about music.

They stop on the steps into the concert hall.

So you see? We don't know each other.

She laughs. She glances at her watch.

I've got to go now.

Embarrassed silence. They shake hands.

You make me curious.

Thomas does not know what to say.

Promise you won't try and contact me at home.

Thomas nods. She goes up the steps.

EXT. CONCERT HALL. NIGHT

Old Thomas is outside the concert hall, carrying his suitcase. The doors have been planked over. The planks are covered in peeling posters. Thomas examines one of the more recent: THE PURPLE PANTHERS *. . . a photo illustrates a group of old ladies in sequinned gowns. The word* DEMONSTRATION *is written over the picture.*

EXT. CONCERT HALL. NIGHT

Night. Evelyne comes down the concert hall steps and looks around. She is disappointed there's no one there to meet her. She picks up her instrument case and walks off slowly.

Adult Thomas runs up, out of breath. Evelyne is delighted . . . but tries not to show it.

THOMAS

Sorry I'm late.

A group of musicians come laughing out of the hall. They surround Evelyne.

Are you coming for a drink? (*He looks at Thomas.*) Is this your husband?

EVELYNE

No. My brother.

Her remark takes Thomas by surprise.

INT. CAFÉ NIGHT

Thomas and Evelyne are sitting in a smoky café, surrounded by musicians. Thomas is unlike anyone else at the table. She observes him. He stays out of a conversation which is beyond him. They exchange a look.

MUSICIANS
(*off-screen*)

Jazz is obviously going to replace all other forms of music. Our ears will get used to hearing five notes at the same time, instead of three . . .

He turns to Thomas.

What does your brother say?

THOMAS

I . . . I've no idea. I don't possess a record-player.

They stare at him as if he's from Mars. Evelyne smiles at him. She likes him.

EVELYNE

He can't resist a joke.

ANOTHER MUSICIAN

Go on, then, tell us a joke.

THOMAS

But I don't . . .

The others are all waiting. Thomas sighs and decides he has got to tell a joke.

Ask me the time.

At the next table too, everyone has fallen silent.

                    MUSICIAN
Excuse me?

                    THOMAS
The time. Ask me the time.

                    MUSICIAN
Err . . . What time is it? OK?

                    THOMAS
The same time it was yesterday at the same time.

No one laughs.

That was the joke.

Evelyne bursts out laughing at the look on the others' faces. She is bent double with laughter.

EXT. 'LES ROSES' VILLA AND STREET. NIGHT

Old Thomas moves through the darkness of Evelyne's street, carrying his case. The neighbourhood is empty. Wastepaper billows across the pavement. All the way up the street, illuminated numbers on gate posts. Thomas stops outside Evelyne's house. The garden is all overgrown. Most of the shutters are down. The house seems abandoned. He walks slowly up the drive towards the front door, pauses, rings the bell. No reply.

INT. CLOTHES SHOP. DAY

Bell. Adult Thomas pushes the door of a clothes shop and enters. Evelyne examines herself in the mirror: she is trying on a black dress. The Sales Assistant fits it. Evelyne's polka-dot dress is hanging in the fitting room. Thomas approaches. Evelyne spins round explosively.

                    EVELYNE
I'VE HAD ENOUGH! I DON'T WANT TO SEE YOU ANY MORE!

Customers turn and stare. The sales assistants are embarrassed. Thomas takes Evelyne by the hand.

THOMAS

Evelyne! Please!

EVELYNE

LEAVE ME ALONE! IT'S OVER, DO YOU HEAR?

Evelyne shoves Thomas away. Clothes fall to the ground. A Sales Assistant rushes forward to pick them up. Evelyne grabs her bag and runs out.

THOMAS

DARLING!

SALES ASSISTANT

MADAM! MADAM!

Thomas stops her.

THOMAS

I'll catch up with her.

He chases after Evelyne.

INT. CAR. DAY

Thomas bursts out of the shop and jumps into his car. Evelyne is waiting in the car, her eyes glued to the shop. He starts the car.

EVELYNE

Quick! Quick!

Thomas steps on the gas. Evelyne holds on to him. They laugh. They glance back. They are not being followed. They laugh till they're out of breath, like a couple of kids.

How was it?

THOMAS

Not bad. You're gifted.

She examines her new dress.

Were you scared?

EVELYNE

Was I scared?! I've never done anything like that! You're out of your mind.

She turns serious.

Damn. I left the other dress in the fitting-room.

She looks back.

My husband gave it to me. I have to go back and . . .

Thomas is laughing.

THOMAS

Leave it there. It's fine.

They stop at a red light. They look at each other earnestly.

You know what is happening?

Evelyne is staring at the traffic lights.

EVELYNE

It's green.

Thomas doesn't take his eyes off her. People sound their horns.

Yes. I know.

They drive on. Evelyne looks at Thomas.

I don't want to fall in love with you.

Evelyne stares at Thomas's mouth.

I don't want to kiss you.

As Thomas drives along, she gives him a long kiss on the lips. Thomas closes his eyes. A horn sounds. Thomas opens his eyes again and jerks the wheel to avoid an on-coming car.

EXT. INSTITUTE FOR THE MENTALLY HANDICAPPED. DAY

Thomas's car stops at the gates. Evelyne emerges from the car, somewhat surprised. She sees a group of patients playing on the lawn.

EVELYNE

Where have you brought me?

THOMAS

I want you to meet my family.

They walk on to the lawn. Célestin is lying in the grass, looking up at the sun. He is smiling. His eyes are shut. Thomas signals to Evelyne that she should wait for a moment. He sits beside Célestin. Célestin does not open his eyes.

CÉLESTIN

I'm glad you've come.

THOMAS

I'm glad too.

Célestin gives a broad grin. He is delighted.

CÉLESTIN

What time is it?

Thomas looks at his watch.

THOMAS

Three minutes to four.

CÉLESTIN

Tea's at four.

THOMAS

Célestin, I'd like you to meet someone.

CÉLESTIN

She's here, now.

THOMAS

Who?

CÉLESTIN

The mole. She's just below. I'm following her along. I can feel her with my back.

THOMAS

Célestin . . .

Thomas runs his hand through his hair. Célestin is stroking the grass.

CÉLESTIN

Grass tickles a bit. And it prickles.

THOMAS

Célestin . . . I want you to meet Evelyne.

Célestin opens his eyes. Evelyne looks at him with surprise.

CÉLESTIN

Is she your girlfriend?

Célestin stands up and takes Evelyne in his arms and gives her a good, long hug. Evelyne doesn't really know what to do. In the end, she hugs him back.

I'm glad.

He takes Evelyne's hand and puts it to his cheek.

A bell rings. The patients move off towards a building. A nurse approaches Célestin.

NURSE

It's time.

CÉLESTIN
(*to Evelyne*)

Don't you want to stay? It's nice here. We don't work or anything. The food is good.

They give each other a smile. Thomas kisses Célestin and goes off with Evelyne. He signals to Evelyne that she should wait. He turns round and returns to Célestin. He takes his head in his hands. Their foreheads touch.

THOMAS

See anything special?

CÉLESTIN

What?

THOMAS

Does she look like Alice?

CÉLESTIN

Who?

THOMAS

Her.

Not at all. She's nothing like her.

Thomas laughs uproariously. Célestin does too, happy that Thomas is happy. They hug and raise each other off the ground like two bears dancing. The bell rings in the distance.

EXT. 'LES ROSES' VILLA. NIGHT

Old Thomas rings at the door insistently. He waits outside Evelyne's house. No reply.

He spots a shed at the bottom of the garden.

INT. GARDEN SHED. NIGHT

Thomas pushes the door of the shed and uses his lighter for a light. He makes room among the mess of tools, sits down and lights a cigarette. He removes the tattered book from his pocket and reads by the light of his lighter. The words run by: 'I often have this dream . . .'

> OLD THOMAS
> (*voice-over*)
' . . . this strange and poignant dream . . .'

INT. THOMAS'S APARTMENT. DAY

Thomas and Evelyne lying on the bed, fully dressed. She strokes his cheek.

> YOUNG THOMAS
> (*voice-over*)
' . . . of a unknown woman whom I love and who loves me. And she is never quite the same nor . . .'

INT. MORGUE. DAY

Scissors cut the corpse's clothes so as to free its arm. A nurse's hand rubs the arm with a damp sponge glove. The action is shown is slow motion.

INT. THOMAS'S APARTMENT. DAY

Thomas and Evelyne kiss. They are naked under the sheets . . .

Evelyne's hair falls over Thomas's face.

INT. GARDEN SHED. NIGHT

Old Thomas stares at Evelyne's house through the open door.

> OLD THOMAS
> (*voice-over*)

'. . . Is she dark or fair or auburn? I cannot tell. Her name? I know it is gentle and resonant, like those of the loved ones banished by life. Her gaze is as a statue's . . .'

INT. THOMAS'S APARTMENT. DAY

Adult Thomas and Evelyne rolling on top of each other and kissing. The sheets tie themselves in knots around them.

> OLD THOMAS
> (*voice-over*)

'. . . And her voice is distant and tranquil and deep, like the tones of loved ones fallen quiet.'

Thomas rolls on his side and goes still. Evelyne puts her head on his shoulder. She raises a hand above his head and watches it against the ceiling.

> EVELYNE

Do you like my hands?

> THOMAS

Yes.

> EVELYNE

Which do you prefer?

Thomas does not reply.

What about my feet. Are they too big?

Thomas turns his head. Evelyne watches him. His back is to her.

Thomas?

> THOMAS

Shut up.

EVELYNE

What have I said?

She tries to get him to look round. He won't. He seems sad. He sits on the bed.

THOMAS

Nothing.

EVELYNE

Look at me.

He looks at her. She's had enough.

I'm me! I can't help it if I remind you of someone! It's me here. Me and no one else.

He gets up and goes into the bathroom.

INT. BATHROOM. DAY

Thomas lies down in the bath, head under water. He does not move. His eyes are open. Ripples at the surface distort his face. He takes his head out of the water.

EVELYNE'S VOICE
(*through the door*)
Thomas? I've got to go . . . Open up . . .

Thomas looks sad. Sound of the door-handle going down. But the door is locked.

EVELYNE
Thomas?

Thomas does not reply.

INT. THOMAS'S APARTMENT. DAY

Thomas comes out of the bathroom. His eyes sweep the room . . . Evelyne gone. The bed is unmade. Thomas sits on the bed. Someone rings at the door.

THOMAS
Who is it?

Thomas doesn't know what to do. He opens the door. Evelyne jumps into his arms. She is crying. He hugs her. She kisses him.

EVELYNE
I want to live with you! I want us to go away! Miles away!

INT. GARDEN SHED. NIGHT

Old Thomas snaps the ammunition cartridge into his gun. Through the open door, he stares at the drive up to the house. He takes aim. Then he puts the gun down and waits.

INT. THOMAS'S APARTMENT. DAY

Two removal men take the last bits of furniture out of Adult Thomas's apartment. Thomas is on the phone.

THOMAS
The flight to New York . . . Yes. I'm confirming two seats . . .

EXT. CONCERT HALL. DAY

Thomas stands beside his car. He is waiting outside the concert hall.

Thomas waits at the wheel of his car. There is a large suitcase on the back seat. No one comes. He looks at his watch and starts the car.

The car drives off. Evelyne appears, carrying a suitcase. She looks around.

EXT. 'LES ROSES' VILLA. DAY

Thomas parks outside Evelyne's house. He stops to think. He walks up the drive and rings the bell. The door opens. Thomas is astonished . . . Alfred is at the door. Alfred is surprised too. He smiles.

> ALFRED
> Thomas! I'd given up expecting you . . . Funny you should turn up today. I . . . I'm not very well.

Alfred looks the worse for wear. His eyes are red. He is unshaven.

> Come in a sec.

Thomas cannot believe this. He follows him inside.

INT. 'LES ROSES' VILLA. DAY

Thomas looks around. Through a half-open door, he sees an empty wardrobe, a few dresses piled up on a bed.

> ALFRED
> Don't mind the mess. My wife is leaving me.

Thomas looks at Alfred. Alfred stands beside a small fountain, watching an ice-cube drift in his whisky.

> I'm told it happens in all the best families . . .

Thomas pauses at the mantelpiece. Under a clock, he finds a framed photograph of Evelyne and Alfred, smiling happily. Evelyne is wearing a white dress and a band in her hair. She looks like Alice. There is also an older series of portraits of Evelyne. Her hair was red. She wore glasses. Then her hair turns dark and the style is Alice's. Then she starts wearing the blue and white dress. Thomas is fascinated by the oldest

*picture of all, which shows a completely different woman, with red hair
and a shy look.*

It takes years to perfect a woman . . . And then when it
happens, she just vanishes.

*Thomas looks at Alfred, whose back is turned. Alfred takes an old white
artificial flower out of his pocket. He twists it in his fingers. It's the
flower Alice made. Alfred stares at it sadly. A tear trickles down his nose
and drops onto the flower.*

INT. LIVING-ROOM. DAY

*Quick flashes: Young Thomas comes into the living-room. Alice laughs.
Young Alfred is in the armchair. Alice stops laughing as she sees
Thomas. Alfred hides the artificial rose from Thomas's eyes.*

INT. 'LES ROSES' VILLA. DAY

*Thomas stares at the flower. He can't believe this. He looks at the photo
in which Evelyne looks so like Alice. He turns to Alfred.*

INT. 'LES ROSES' VILLA. DAY

Flash: Thomas drowns Alfred in the fountain.

INT. 'LES ROSES' VILLA. DAY

*Alfred examines the artificial flower. Thomas backs towards the door,
aghast. He runs away.*

INT. STATION. DAY

*Thomas runs through the station. He chucks two plane tickets into a
bin. He stops, breathlessly, before the indicator board. He runs his finger
over the different destinations, with his eyes closed. His finger stops. He
sees the word 'Mauville'. He runs to buy a ticket.*

EXT. PLATFORM. DAY

*Thomas waits on a bench. He is in tears. Beside him, a cigarette
machine. He puts some coins in. He asks a passer-by for a light.*

INT. TRAIN COMPARTMENT. DAY

Thomas inhales the cigarette smoke. Tears come to his eyes. He coughs. On the next seat, a Young Man watches him. He looks severe. He wears spectacles. He looks rather like Thomas did a few weeks earlier.

> YOUNG MAN
> Excuse me, this is a non-smoking carriage.

Thomas ignores him.

> Do you know, 60 per cent of all cancers are caused by cigarette smoke?

Thomas leaps on the Young Man and beats him up. The Young Man yells. They roll on to the floor. Passengers start shouting. A conductor appears and separates them. The other passenger is picked up. Thomas remains on the floor, sobbing and shaking every time the train shudders. His tears turn to laughter. Old Thomas's laughter (off-screen) mixes in with his.

INT. MORGUE CORRIDOR, NIGHT

The corpse rolls on a trolley down a long corridor. The corpse shakes every time the trolley shudders. The head shifts beneath the cloth.

> OLD THOMAS
> (*voice-over*)
> 'Out, out, brief candle! Life's but a walking shadow, a poor player that struts and frets his hour upon the stage, and then is heard no more; it is a tale told by an idiot, full of sound and fury, signifying NOTHING!' *Macbeth*, act 5, scene 5 . . . Ha ha ha!

INT. MORGUE. NIGHT

A metal door slides open to reveal a tray. The corpse slides in. The heavy metal door clangs shut.

INT. GARDEN SHED. NIGHT

The wind blows the shed door several times. Old Thomas has fallen asleep. His gun hangs in his hand. Sound of steps on the gravel.

EXT. 'LES ROSES' VILLA. NIGHT

Toto's car is parked at the bottom, on the street. Toto moves cautiously up the drive, gun in hand, until he reaches the gangster's Jag. He steps on something that makes a sound. He bends down and picks up a sweet-wrapper. A tune comes in from the ground-floor windows, which are all lit up . . .

FATHER'S VOICE
Glug-glug-glug go the turkeys
and the lovely bell rings ding-a-ling-ling . . .

Toto comes up to the windows. He gets ready and . . .

INT. 'LES ROSES' VILLA. NIGHT

The window shatters. Toto bursts into the room, gun in hand. There is no one there. A record on a turntable plays a piano version of 'Boom' . . .

Suddenly, six Gangsters armed to the teeth burst in with a machine-gun. Their Boss looks uncannily like Adult Alfred.

BOSS
Surprise! Surprise! Van Chickensoup!

Toto goes pale at the name. The Gangsters laugh and take up the refrain.

GANGSTERS
VAN-CHI-CKEN-SOUP-VAN-CHI-SCKEN-SOUP . . .

Toto is livid, his eyes popping out of their sockets. His lips tremble. In one giant leap, he jumps up and starts shooting all over the room.

TOTO
(*yelling*)
MY NAME IS NOT VAN CHICKENSOUP! MY
NAME IS NOT VAN CHICKENSOUP!

Bullets shatter everything: vases, glass-cases, plasterwork. All the windows are pulverized, the cupboards splayed open. Gangsters fall to the ground. Blood sprays out of their bellies. They fall in heaps. A red tide spreads over the parquet floor.

TOTO

My name is not Van Chickensoup . . .

The Boss sneaks out of a door. Toto chases after him.

INT. CLOTHES SHOP. DAY

A door on to the back of the shop. Toto sees the gangster vanish behind a pile of clothes. Toto hides, then sneaks forwards. In the background, a Sales Assistant is talking to Alfred and Evelyne. Evelyne tries on a dress.

ALFRED

That isn't it. We need something wider, with shorter sleeves.

SALES ASSISTANT

Well, you certainly know what you want.

EVELYNE

But I like this one!

Toto edges forward, gun in hand. The Sales Assistant returns with a blue and white dress, identical to Alice's.

ALFRED

That's exactly it.

The Gangster shoves Alfred out of the way and rushes for the door. Toto leaps forwards and shoots. Alfred is wounded in the chest. He falls to the floor. Yells. The Gangster shoots at Toto. Toto is wounded in the shoulder.

INT. GARDEN SHED. NIGHT

Old Thomas wakes with a start. He tries to calm his breathing. The gun is still in his hand. Whispering wakes him up. Outside, it's too dark to see. But there are voices. Thomas tries to listen. He holds his breath so as not to make a sound. He moves silently to the wall. Between the planks, he sees a man squat down.

EXT. 'LES ROSES' VILLA (POV: THOMAS). NIGHT

Legs of two men squatting down beside the shed.

MAN I
(*whispers*)
. . . from here, I can get at him . . .

*Shoes . . . in the darkness, a tripod stuck in the ground . . . a rifle sight
. . . Man 1 leans towards Man 2.*

MAN 2
(*whispers*)
When he comes in . . . See the second window, there? The
shutter's stuck, it always stays open . . . Just by the phone.
You'll hear the bell . . .

The two men move away with the rifle.

INT./EXT. GARDEN SHED. NIGHT

*Thomas's eyes, wide with astonishment, between the planks. He dares
not make a sound.*

EXT. 'LES ROSES' VILLA STREET. NIGHT

*Thomas runs with his case. He glances back anxiously to see if he's
being followed.*

EXT. THOMAS'S STREET AND KANT HOUSE. DAWN

*The sun rises. It has been raining. Thomas's coat is soaking wet.
Thomas appears in the street he used to live in as a child. The
neighbourhood is deserted. Most of the houses look abandoned. There
are hoardings for abandoned building sites. A dog barks in the distance.
On every side, high buildings have grown up around the
neighbourhood. In the distance, television screens broadcast
commercials. Thomas stops outside the Kant house. There is a Jaguar
parked beside it. The shutters are closed. The paint is peeling.*

*Thomas pushes the gate open. He puts his hand in his pocket and
clutches his gun. He goes up three steps to the entrance.*

*Thomas looks at the door. He presses the doorbell. A bell rings. Silence.
Curtains shift at a window. The door opens a fraction. A little man in a
towelling dressing-gown puts his head around the door. He looks at
Thomas with suspicion. He wears spectacles. His hair is white. He is*

hunched over and seems smaller than Thomas.

ALFRED

Can I help you?

Thomas does not reply. Alfred gives him a worried look. Thomas tightens his grasp on his gun. He points it at Alfred through the lining of his trousers.

THOMAS
(*mumbles*)

Bang!

Alfred starts. Thomas laughs. Alfred looks puzzled. Thomas laughs and goes down the steps.

ALFRED

Who are you?

Thomas is on the pavement. He moves away, laughing. Alfred comes out.

What do you want?

Thomas stops and sits on the garden wall of a house next door.

THOMAS?! . . . IT'S YOU?!

Thomas looks at his toes and laughs. A drop of water falls on his shoes. Another drop collects at the tip of his nose, then falls.

Alfred is a few yards from Thomas. He seems apprehensive. He puts his hand on Thomas's shoulder.

Thomas?

Thomas looks up. His eyes are red. He smiles.

THOMAS

Hi, Alfred. You look older.

ALFRED

So do you.

THOMAS

I hear it's the best way not to die young.

INT. KANT HOUSE SITTING-ROOM. DAY

Thomas goes into Alfred's house. The decor is old-fashioned.

ALFRED

Take a seat.

Thomas sits in an armchair which is too low. They look at each other for a time without knowing what to say.

What have you been up to all this time?

THOMAS

I don't know. (*He laughs.*) Probably being what I didn't want to be.

Alfred smiles as if Thomas had cracked a joke.

ALFRED

I'll make you a coffee.

Thomas remains alone. He looks around. On the mantelpiece, a photograph of an old lady. Alfred returns and gives Thomas a cup of coffee. Thomas stirs his coffee. A drop trickles down the spout of the coffee pot.

Remember when you wanted us to swap lives?

Thomas smiles.

I've often wondered how it would have turned out . . . I always envied you. Your life was so much simpler than mine was. I thought you always did exactly as you pleased.

Thomas is surprised at this. He fidgets with his cuff. He is uncomfortable in the low chair. He looks into his coffee cup.

THOMAS

I heard you had some trouble.

ALFRED

I have to make myself scarce for a while. You're the only one who knows where I am. (*He smiles.*) My secret's safe.

Thomas hands him a pack of cigarettes.

I don't smoke any more. My wife got me to give up.

Thomas is somewhat taken aback. Alfred notices this reaction.

I remarried. It wasn't . . . the one you were thinking of.

He looks at Thomas for a long while. Thomas returns his stare. Then he breaks the silence.

I see her sometimes. We've remained friends. (*Pause.*) She left me after you disappeared. She missed you very badly. And I missed her too, for a long, long time.

Thomas's hand is shaking somewhat.

It was later that I found out, when she started mentioning you.

They look at each other in silence. There is no hostility in Alfred's expression.

Would you like to see her?

Thomas sneezes. He is soaked to the skin.

I'll get you a dry coat.

EXT. CITY SQUARE. DAY

Thomas appears on a small square surrounded by disproportionately large buildings. Giant television screen broadcast commercials. An overhead train crosses the square, suspended from a monorail.

In the middle of the square, about fifty old people demonstrate. They carry banners. There is a band on a dais. Thomas reads the banners: 'Stand up for yourselves, Senior Citizens'. Thomas fights his way through the crowd. The old people's band starts playing rock'n'roll. Six old ladies in fishnet stockings perform a wild dance.

OLD LADIES
(*singing*)

We don't want no retirement homes,
Millions like us . . .

Thomas examines the band. He looks at each of the players in turn. He starts when a hand is laid on his shoulder.

214

Thomas?

Thomas turns round. An old lady with white hair looks at him in surprise. She is carrying a banner. Thomas stares at her.

THOMAS

Evelyne?

They look at each other in silence. Evelyne bites her lip. Tears well up in her eyes. She shakes Thomas's hand.

EVELYNE

I waited for you, for such a long time.

Thomas lowers his eyes.

You left so fast, without a word.

Evelyne looks Thomas up and down. She runs her hand across the coat that Alfred lent him.

It looks like America worked out for you.

She smiles. Thomas says nothing. She throws herself in his arms. Thomas hugs her tight. She takes his face in her hands. They kiss; their wrinkled mouths press together. Evelyne looks at him as though she does not believe it can really be him. People bump into them. The crowd around them is packed. They pay no attention. They look at each other. A voice makes them turn round.

EVELYNE'S HUSBAND

Evelyne?

An old gentleman is staring at Evelyne. Evelyne lets go of Thomas.

EVELYNE

I . . . my husband. Wait a minute.

Evelyne goes to her husband. Thomas watches them talking. The man looks overcome. Evelyne tries to calm him down. Thomas feels uneasy.

A sound from the far end of the street. Horses' hoofs. Smoke bombs go off. The crowd backs away, then breaks into a run. Thomas is carried off. His eyes search for Evelyne, but he has lost her.

He backs into a wall (or a church front) to let the crowd by. His watch falls from his wrist and breaks. Thomas picks it up. The glass is smashed, the hands gone. He looks around. The square is empty. He picks up his suitcase.

INT. CHURCH. DAY

Thomas enters an empty church. It has hardly changed. The statue of the Virgin that Alice once knocked over is still there, mended. The crucifix has been unhooked. It is propped on the ground to allow someone to repaint the walls. A painter comes down off a ladder and vanishes into the sacristy. Thomas remains alone. He goes to the crucifix and looks at it. He takes a chair and sits down beside it.

> THOMAS
> We've never had much to say to each other. It's time we had a chat.

Christ, nailed to the cross, looks at him with pity. Thomas falls silent.

A long silence . . .

> I . . .

He falls silent again. He looks around. He stares at the crucifix.

Steps behind him. The painters return, pick up the crucifix and take it away. Thomas watches them go. He stands and takes his case.

EXT. COUNTRY ROAD. DAY

Thomas walks down a country road, which is straight and empty. It is raining hard. His hair is wet. Sound of an engine. Thomas turns round and holds out his thumb. A truck stops. Thomas climbs in.

INT./EXT. TRUCK AND ROAD. DAY

Thomas in the passenger seat. The landscape travels by. Another, ancient, truck overtakes them and stays right in front of them. Thomas stares at the truck. Beside him, the Driver is whistling the Charles Trenet song:

> DRIVER
> Mmmmh mh mmmh mh . . .

Thomas shuts his eyes. He sinks back in his seat. He opens his eyes slowly: the tarpaulin on the truck ahead lifts up. Through the rain on the windscreen, Thomas sees red theatrical curtains on the back of the truck in front. They float in the wind. Thomas's Father stands between the curtains, wearing a black tail-coat, with his hair greased back and a carnation in his buttonhole. He still looks thirty years old. He sings with a tremor in his voice. Beside him, child Alice plays the trumpet.

FATHER
(*singing*)
The clock goes tick-tock, tick-tick,
The birds on the lake go plick-plack, plick-plick,
Glug-glug-glug go the turkeys,
And the lovely bell rings ding-a-ling-ling . . .

The truck gathers speed and moves away, its curtains billowing in the wind. A gust of rain hits the windscreen . . . Thomas's face. The road is empty again.

THOMAS
Stop here!

EXT. COUNTRY ROAD. DAY

Thomas gets out of the truck. It starts up again. Thomas stops. He takes his gun out of his pocket. He looks at it for a moment, wondering what to do. Then he puts it back in his pocket. He turns round and walks back into town.

EXT. KANT HOUSE. DAY

Thomas rings Alfred's door. The door opens a fraction. Alfred is surprised to see him again.

THOMAS
Can I come in?

INT. KANT HOUSE HALL. DAY

Alfred shows Thomas in. He is dripping wet.

THOMAS
Could you make me a coffee?

ALFRED

I . . . Of course.

Alfred heads for the kitchen. Thomas follows him. As soon as Alfred is in there, Thomas closes the door and turns the key in the lock.

ALFRED'S VOICE
(*through the door*)
THOMAS?! . . . What are you doing?

Alfred bangs on the door.

INT. KANT HOUSE BEDROOM. DAY

Thomas shaves himself closely in the mirror.

He carefully combs his hair.

He removes one of Alfred's suits from the wardrobe.

He knots a tie.

He looks at himself in the mirror. He seems elegant.

INT. KANT HOUSE HALL. DAY

Thomas rummages through the pockets of a raincoat on the coatstand: he finds a set of keys.

EXT. THOMAS'S STREET. DAY

Alfred's Jaguar emerges from the garden and drives off. Thomas is at the wheel.

INT. INFANTS' WARD. NIGHT

Swirls of smoke. Baby Thomas in his cot. Mrs Kant runs up. She takes Thomas in her arms and runs away with him.

EXT. 'LES ROSES' VILLA. NIGHT

The streetlights are on in the street. Thomas turns the Jaguar into the drive. It parks outside Alfred's imposing mansion. Thomas in his impeccable suit gets out of the car (silhouette seen from the POV of someone watching). Thomas tries the keys. The door opens.

INT. 'LES ROSES' VILLA. NIGHT

Thomas goes into the living-room. The furniture is covered in dust-sheets. Thomas tries a switch. A small fountain goes on. A second switch. The lights go on.

EXT. 'LES ROSES' VILLA. NIGHT

From the street, Thomas's silhouette in the window the shutter of which does not close.

Toto staggers through the trees. His shoulder is bleeding. He hides behind a tree trunk. He sees Old Thomas's silhouette in the window. Slowly, he takes aim . . .

INT. 'LES ROSES' VILLA. NIGHT

Old Thomas goes to the mantelpiece. Under a glass sphere there is Alice's white artificial rose, now yellowed. Thomas lifts up the sphere. He takes the rose and twists it in his fingers.

On the desk, a glass bowl full of red sweets. The same kind as the Father used to do his magic tricks with. Thomas takes one.

The phone rings. Thomas goes to the window. He raises the receiver a fraction and lets it drop. He turns his back to the window. He does not move any more.

EXT. 'LES ROSES'. VILLA. NIGHT

Thomas's silhouette clearly outlined in the window.

Toto aims at Thomas. He turns around . . . Behind him, a car passes in the street and dazzles him . . . Suspense music . . .

INT. 'LES ROSES' VILLA. NIGHT

Headlights light up a wall. Thomas's gaze follows the rectangle of light moving across the wall till it reaches the portrait of Mr Kant . . . Thomas looks at Kant's smiling face.

THOMAS

Bye, Dad.

Thomas unwraps his sweet. He puts it in his mouth. He shuts his eyes, very slowly, as though going to sleep. A shot. The window shatters around a small hole: a bullet hole. Shining glass showers down. Thomas turns on himself and crumples . . .

EXT. 'LES ROSES' VILLA. NIGHT

Toto has been hit in the back. He turns himself and crumples . . . The two motions combine.

INT. 'LES ROSES' VILLA. NIGHT

Thomas is caught in the curtain. It winds round his neck. In slow motion, Thomas's face falls into the fountain. Sweets scatter over the ground, like a pearl necklace breaking.

INT. 'LES ROSES' VILLA. NIGHT

Police sirens. Photographic flashes. Thomas's motionless corpse on the ground. He is dragged out of the water and turned over. He seems to be smiling . . .

INT. MORGUE. DAY

The metallic door is opened. Alfred comes forward. He is moved. He removes his hat. An inspector accompanies him. The corpse's face is discovered: Thomas's face. Cut out against the ceiling, Alfred bends over him. Thomas's face seems to be smiling, even in death. Alfred turns to the inspector and nods.

INT. INSPECTOR'S OFFICE. DAY

The inspector is at his desk, examining clues: the artificial rose, the sweets, the broken watch. He puts the lot into a cardboard box.

INT. ARCHIVES. DAY

A trolley rolls past shelving. Among other cardboard files, it contains one marked 'VAN HASEBROECK THOMAS'. The trolley disappears among the shelves loaded with box files.

EXT. MORGUE STREET. DAY

The door of a car slams closed. The brand-name CHEVROLET *appears.*

> OLD THOMAS
> (*voice-over*)
> I've always wanted a Chevrolet . . .

The car drives off. It is a hearse.

INT. CREMATORIUM. DAY

Flames. Wind gusting. The coffin creaks forward mechanically. The doors close on it with great solemnity. A loudspeaker hanging from a nail broadcasts a requiem to cover the sound of the flames.

In the crematorium, Alfred stands alone among empty benches. He blows his nose and leaves. Alone.

INT. CREMATORIUM BACK-ROOM. DAY

A tray of steaming ashes is removed. A poker rummages through the ashes. They are transferred to a small plastic bag upon which a label is stuck.

INT. ROOM IN A RETIREMENT HOME. DAY

A cleaning lady and a nurse clear out Old Thomas's room in the retirement home. They put his belongings into a cardboard box.

INT. AUCTION-HOUSE. DAY

Thomas's objects in a pile on a tray. A frame containing a photograph of Alice is visible, along with a reel of 8mm film and various small objects.

> AUCTIONEER
> (*off-screen*)
> Various small objects, one lot, starting price twenty francs . . .
> ten francs . . . 5 francs . . .

The hammer goes down.

EXT. AIRPORT RUNWAY. DAY

A pilot walks towards a private plane, carrying a cardboard box. He puts it on the passenger seat.

The propeller starts to turn. The plane moves forwards and takes off.

INT. PLANE. DAY

In the cardboard box, various plastic bags piled up. They are full of black dust. The label on the top bag is marked '006-58336 THOMAS VAN HASEBROECK'.

OLD THOMAS
(voice-over; laughing)

Ha ha ha! That's it! I'M FLYING! HA HA!

Through a bit of window, clouds go by.

EXT. ABOVE THE CLOUDS. DAY

The plane arrives above the clouds. A white mattress extends as far as the eye can see. The sun shines.

OLD THOMAS
(voice-over)

Oooooooooh!

INT. PLANE. DAY

The pilot's hand reaches uncertainly for the box and grabs the bag marked 'THOMAS VAN HASEBROECK'. The pilot opens a side window. The wind blows in. With his spare hand, he brings the bag to his teeth and tears it open. He reaches out of the window . . .

OLD THOMAS
(voice-over)

HEEEEEEY!

Dust escapes from the bag and leaves a black trail.

EXT. SKY AND COUNTRY. DAY

The plastic flies off along the body of the plane. Wind blows into it, sending it into a spin. Thomas laughs as if he was being tickled.

> OLD THOMAS
> (*voice-over*)

Aaaah! . . . Oh! Hihihi!

The bag spins up. The ground comes close. Houses seem tiny. A truck drives by, looking like a toy. The dust vanishes into the air. The bag empties.

EXT. LOW ALTITUDE, COUNTRY. DAY

The ground nears. Two lovers kissing in a field, thinking no one can see them. A bicyclist passes near them, noticing. The click of his chain.

EXT. LOW ALTITUDE, THOMAS'S STREET. DAY

Above a group of houses: Thomas's childhood neighbourhood. In the backyard of one of the houses, an old man appears surreptitiously. This is Alfred.

> OLD THOMAS
> (*voice-over*)

HEY! ALFRED! ALFRED! I'M UP HERE!

Alfred moves quickly to the bottom of his garden and rights a flower-pot that has been turned over. Underneath, there is a packet of cigarettes.

Ha ha ha!

EXT. LOW ALTITUDE, COUNTRY. DAY

Fields. A road . . . a car . . . Evelyne in the car. Her son is driving . . . There's a banner on the roof-rack marked 'Stand up, Senior Citizens!' . . . They are smiling . . .

Flying over fields, the ground approaches . . . Thomas's laughter grows more distant . . . The picture turns very light, overexposed, then lands in grass. Music from afar. A voice singing:

> VOICE

The clock goes tick-tock, tick-tock,
The birds on the lake go plick-plack, plick-plick . . .

EXT. GROUND, COUNTRY. DAY

Ducks in the sunshine . . .

> VOICE
> Glug-glug-glug go the turkeys . . .

A turkey chick runs behind a mother turkey . . .

A steeple in the distance . . .

> VOICE
> And the lovely bell rings ding-a-ling-ling
> But boom!

Lovers kissing in the fields . . .

> When the heart goes BOOM!
> Everything else goes BOOM!
> And love starts a-stirring . . .
> (etc.)

A few specks of dust fall on a white garden table. A woman's hand passes a cloth over them and shakes them out a few yards away.

> OLD THOMAS
> (*voice-over*)
> Ha ha ha!

The laughter is distant now. A few specks of dust fall in a grassy field. A cow's nose comes up and eats the grass.

> Moooooo!

The plastic bag drops in a river and hangs on a fallen branch. Water streams between stones . . . Everything goes white and bright.